PRIMARY
PROBLEM SOLVING
IN MATH

101 Activities

Jack A. Coffland, Ph.D.
Winthrop College

Gilbert J. Cuevas, Ph.D.
University of Miami

Illustrated by Toni Summers

GoodYearBooks
An Imprint of ScottForesman
A Division of HarperCollins*Publishers*

Book design by Amy O'Brien Krupp.

GoodYearBooks
are available for most basic curriculum subjects plus many enrichment areas. For more
GoodYearBooks, contact your local bookseller or educational dealer. For a complete catalog
with information about other GoodYearBooks, please write:

GoodYearBooks
ScottForesman
1900 East Lake Avenue
Glenview, IL 60025

ISBN 0-673-38745-3

1 2 3 4 5 6 7 8 9 10 - MAC - 01 00 99 98 97 96 95 94 93 92

TABLE OF CONTENTS

Chapter 2

Situational Problems 53

Instructional Considerations 54

Activity Objectives 55

Teaching Suggestions: Discussion Activities

Chapter 3

Algorithmic Problems 73

Instructional Considerations 74

Activity Objectives 75

Activities and Teaching Suggestions

Chapter 4

Transitional Activities   111

Chapter 5

Information Gathering and Processing 156

Instructional Considerations 156

Activity Objectives 157

Activities and Teaching Suggestions

From *Primary Problem Solving in Math* by Jack A. Coffland and Gilbert J. Cuevas. Copyright © 1992 by GoodYearBooks.

INTRODUCTION

Problem Solving and the Mathematics Curriculum

A reform movement is underway in the way we teach mathematics: It is evident in the ideas and recommendations presented in the National Council of Teachers of Mathematics' *Curriculum and Evaluation Standards for School Mathematics* (1989). The move is toward a curriculum that emphasizes building conceptual understanding and problem-solving abilities rather than rote memorization. Mathematics educators are being challenged to make the transition from current classroom practice to the instructional orientations recommended in the *Standards.*

We have prepared *Primary Problem Solving in Math* as a framework to help you in making this transition. The instructional ideas, suggestions, and activities it contains are intended as tools you can use in developing children's problem-solving skills. The book's content is based on five assumptions:

1. Problem solving should provide the organizational framework for the mathematics curriculum in the elementary grades.

    We need to educate students who can think critically and logically. At the turn of the new century, it will be more important than ever for students to know what questions to ask rather than to give answers to all the questions that are posed. Consequently, curricular emphasis on rote, mechanical processes must giv way to thinking, exploration, and communication. It is time for all mathematics educators, from kindergarten to college, to turn toward a curriculum based upon problem solving that can help children become proficient critical thinkers.

2. The development of skills related to the understanding and solution of non-routine problems must be a goal of the mathematics curriculum.

There is general agreement concerning the conditions that make a problem non-routine:

a. there are no readily available steps for the solution,

b. creative thought is required,

c. previous knowledge plays a role in the solution, and

d. this knowledge must be synthesized and applied to the problem situation to reach a conclusion.

The mathematics program in any classroom is not complete until students have had many experiences in solving non-routine problems.

3. Many of the skills used to solve routine problems can be transferred to the solution of non-routine problems.

Routine problems, commonly known as the "story" problems found in mathematics textbooks, stress the use of a previously learned set of steps for their solution. Does the present emphasis upon non-routine problems mean that children no longer have to solve the traditional, routine problems presented in math texts?

Our answer is no. Routine problems can emphasize the skills that should be learned in order to solve non-routine problems. Among these skills are:

■ identification of necessary problem information, including evaluation of data as missing or irrelevant,

■ identification and interpretation of the problem question,

■ "translation" of problem information to the numerical expressions or processes used in the solution, and

■ thinking of the problem by means of a picture or diagram.

All the above skills are used in the solution of non-routine problems. If approached appropriately, routine problems can be useful in helping children build problem-solving abilities.

4. Students' acquisition of problem-solving skills is best achieved through active involvement in a variety of problem-solving situations.

Children develop problem-solving skills through experience. Therefore, they should be exposed to many situations that actively engage them in problem-solving opportunities.

In mathematics, manipulatives facilitate this involvement. The use of concrete materials can help students develop an understanding of a problem as they visualize its conditions and make the necessary connection between the problem situation and what they already know. The use of concrete objects also helps students verbalize their own problem-solving activities. The teacher's role is to make these materials available to students, to guide children through the understanding of problems using the objects, and to assist students in making the transition from the concrete to the abstract.

5. Language skills play an important role in teaching about and learning how to problem solve.

According to Driscoll (1980), "Mathematics is no one's native language, and so no one thinks or communicates totally in mathematics. Yet, more than any other discipline, mathematics requires careful translation, much as any foreign language does. If the translation breaks down, misconceptions grow and mathematical thinking suffers." (p. 31)

Indeed, students must master the meanings of words associated with mathematical functions. Further, language plays a role in developing problem-solving skills. Reading ability is needed in order to:

■ understand the problem as given in the problem statement,

■ identify necessary data to solve the problem, and

■ determine and interpret the question or requirements given in the problem.

Language skills act as the bridge for students to connect verbal with symbolic or mathematical processes. And, of course, language skills are necessary for students to communicate how a problem was solved. Language skills are part of the total process of learning to be an effective problem solver.

Problem Solving and *Primary Problem Solving in Math*

The topics addressed in *Primary Problem Solving in Math* follow George Polya's general guidelines for problem solving. Polya was a noted mathematician who made the study and teaching of problem solving one of his life's professional and personal goals. In 1945, he published *How to Solve It*, his first paper on the process of problem solving. According to Polya, this process involves the following steps:

1. Understanding the problem
2. Devising a plan for solving the problem using the data given and the questions posed
3. Carrying out the plan to solve the problem
4. Checking the answer obtained

We have addressed these steps in problem solving by focusing *Primary Problem Solving in Math* on five major topics: heuristic problems, situational problems, algorithmic problems, transitional activities, and information-gathering activities.

Problem Solving Framework

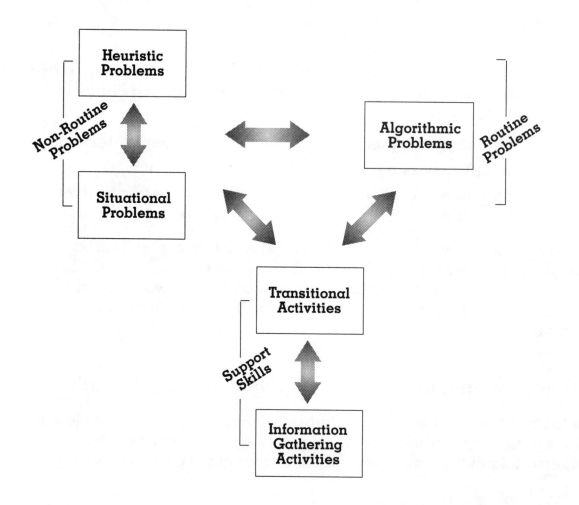

Chapter Organization

Chapter One presents a discussion of non-routine (heuristic) problems and the role they play in mathematical problem solving. Heuristic problems can be viewed as those problems for which the student has no immediate solution procedure. It must be created, invented, or discovered as the student works on the problem. The ultimate goal of mathematics instruction is to help students solve these kinds of problems. Instructional suggestions in this chapter emphasize techniques and activities for teaching students different strategies for solving heuristic problems.

Chapter Two deals with real-life problems that require multiple steps and alternatives in order to reach a solution. The problem-solving process includes: a consideration of the factors that might affect the problem, an evaluation of how these factors may affect a solution, and arrival at a conclusion or solution based upon all the previous steps. Suggestions for teachers and instructional activities emphasize the process of problem solving, not the outcome which is characteristic of algorithmic problems.

The third chapter focuses upon algorithmic problems, those problems that require the child to select and use a previously internalized series of steps (an algorithm) to solve the problem correctly. These are the traditional "story" problems included in most elementary mathematics textbooks. Suggestions are given in this chapter for both a systematic approach to the teaching of "story" problems and for integration of some of the skills addressed by these problems into a non-routine problem-solving scheme.

Chapter Four offers suggestions and classroom activities for helping students make the transition from numerical and computational contexts which are emphasized at the primary level to the verbal contexts in which problems will eventually be given. This transitional process uses the child's experiences to provide meaning to the numerical skills that are to be acquired.

The last chapter addresses the reading skills necessary for problem solving. Activities include identifying information from situational contexts, understanding and using math vocabulary, and identifying and interpreting the problem question. This chapter also focuses on "information processing"— what students do cognitively using information derived from the problem statement and connecting it with previous knowledge. Instructional strategies and activities are presented in this chapter to help students acquire these "information processing" skills.

The sum of these chapters represents our approach to problem solving instruction. However, it is neither a sequence nor a hierarchy. Choose activities selectively and in an order that seems appropriate as you meet each child's needs. For example, a child who one day completes transitional number activities may spend the next day solving heuristic problems. Or, a child who is being introduced to algorithmic problems may need to spend time working with information-gathering activities in order to read a problem more effectively. Our book presents a menu, not a prescription, of strategies and activities for you to select from in developing the problem-solving abilities of individual students.

Chapter Features

Introduction: First, each problem-solving topic is defined; suggestions for instructional strategies and objectives for activities follow.

Student Activities: This section provides activities for each of the skills identified. Each activity includes a short lesson followed by exercises and/or problems that require students to apply what they have just learned. Instructional suggestions and strategies are provided for each of the activities whenever appropriate. Use the chart on pages 7–9 to help you in assessing the difficulty of each worksheet and its most appropriate grade level. In making your determination, you also will want to take into account the skill level and maturity of the children with whom you are working.

Sources

Driscoll, M. *Research Within Reach: A Research-Guided Response to the Concern of Educators*. St. Louis, MO: CEMREL, Inc., 1980.

National Council of Teachers of Mathematics. *Curriculum and Evaluation Standards for School Mathematics*. Reston, VA: National Council of Teachers of Mathematics, 1989.

Polya, G. *How to Solve It*. Princeton, NJ: Princeton University Press, 1945.

Activity Grade Level Chart

Chap/ Act. #	Activity	Suggested Grade level				Page
		K	1	2	3	
1-1	Finger Addition	■	■			14
1-2	Clues to the Unknown			■	■	15
1-3	Square Challenge	■	■	■		17
1-4	Writing Sentences with Numbers		■			19
1-5	Start Your Calculators		■	■		21
1-6	Name That Shape, Part 1	■	■			23
1-7	Name That Shape, Part 2	■	■			25
1-8	What Comes Next?	■	■			27
1-9	Mystery Numbers		■			29
1-10	Fun With Beads	■	■			31
1-11	Thinking of Everything!			■	■	33
1-12	The Five Little Pigs Go Home			■	■	35
1-13	Building a Ten		■			37
1-14	Coin Countdown	■				39
1-15	Calculator Capers			■	■	41
1-16	Triangle Puzzle			■		43
1-17	Valuable Shapes, Part 1			■	■	45
1-18	Valuable Shapes, Part 2			■	■	47
1-19	Valuable Shapes, Part 3			■	■	49
1-20	Building a Toy			■	■	51
2-21	The Cupcake Dilemma	■	■			56
2-22	The Peanut Butter Sandwich	■	■			57
2-23	Vegetable Soup	■	■			58
2-24	Just One Computer	■	■			59
2-25	Getting Ready for School	■	■			59
2-26	Not Enough Water	■	■			60
2-27	A Classroom Pet	■	■			60
2-28	Our Field Trip to the Zoo	■	■			61
2-29	Our Valentine's Day Party	■	■			61
2-30	Sharing Blocks	■	■			62
2-31	A Bagful of Problems	■	■			62
2-32	Planning a Field Trip			■	■	65
2-33	Scouting Outing			■		67
2-34	Happy Birthday			■	■	69

Activity Grade Level Chart Cont'd.

Chap/ Act. #	Activity	Suggested Grade level				Page
		K	1	2	3	
2-35	A Valentine Gift	▓	▓	▓	▓	71
3-36	All About Teddy Bears (addition)	▓	▓			76
3-37	Adding With Cubes	▓	▓			77
3-38	Dinosaur Countdown (addition)	▓	▓			78
3-39	Dinosaur Dash (subtraction)	▓	▓			81
3-40	Blockbusters (subtraction)	▓	▓			82
3-41	Subtracting with Cubes	▓	▓			83
3-42	More About Teddy Bears (addition/subtraction)	▓	▓	▓		85
3-43	More Blockbusters (addition/subtraction)	▓	▓	▓		86
3-44	Tile Tactics (addition/subtraction)	▓	▓	▓		87
3-45	How Many More? (subtraction)		▓	▓	▓	89
3-46	The Missing Addend (subtraction)		▓	▓	▓	91
3-47	Using Questions to Find Answers (add./sub.)		▓	▓	▓	93
3-48	Putting Things in Order (subtraction)		▓	▓	▓	94
3-49	Finding Hidden Numbers		▓	▓	▓	97
3-50	Extra! Extra!		▓	▓	▓	99
3-51	Problem-Solving Pictures	▓	▓	▓	▓	101
3-52	Learning About Multiplication			▓	▓	103
3-53	Learning More About Multiplication			▓	▓	105
3-54	Let's Go Fly a Kite (addition/subtraction)			▓	▓	107
3-55	Party Time (multiplication)			▓	▓	108
4-56	Look Alikes	▓	▓	▓		117
4-57	Look Out!		▓	▓		119
4-58	Making a Match		▓	▓		121
4-59	Which Set is Different?		▓	▓		123
4-60	Addition Number Sentences	▓	▓	▓		126
4-61	Subtraction as Take-Away		▓	▓		127
4-62	Subtraction as Comparison		▓	▓	▓	128
4-63	Subtraction as Missing Addend		▓	▓	▓	129
4-64	Multiplication as Repeated Addition	▓	▓	▓	▓	130
4-65	Multiplication as a Cartesian Product		▓	▓	▓	131
4-66	Division as Measurement Division	▓	▓	▓	▓	132
4-67	Division as Partition		▓	▓	▓	133
4-68	Combining Sets	▓	▓	▓		134

From *Primary Problem Solving in Math* by Jack A. Coffland and Gilbert J. Cuevas. Copyright © 1992 by GoodYearBooks.

Activity Grade Level Chart Cont'd.

Chap/ Act. #	Activity	Suggested Grade level				Page
		K	1	2	3	
4-69	Building Number Sentences About Addition		▓	▓		136
4-70	Writing Number Sentences About Addition		▓	▓		138
4-71	Learning About Subtraction as Take Away		▓	▓		140
4-72	Building Number Sentences About Sub.		▓	▓		142
4-73	Practice with Addition		▓	▓		144
4-74	Practice with Subtraction		▓	▓		145
4-75	Adding and Subtracting Together		▓	▓		146
4-76	Labeling Answers		▓	▓		147
4-77	Picturing Problems		▓	▓		148
4-78	Thinking About Math Questions (add.)		▓	▓		149
4-79	Thinking About Math Questions (sub.)		▓	▓		150
4-80	What's the Right Sign?		▓	▓		151
4-81	Practice Makes Perfect		▓	▓		152
4-82	Following Directions		▓	▓		153
5-83	Linking Numbers with Experience	▓	▓	▓	▓	158
5-84	Making Comparisons	▓	▓			160
5-85	Making Numerical Comparisons	▓	▓			162
5-86	Linking Symbols and Words (addition)		▓	▓		164
5-87	Linking Symbols and Words (subtraction)		▓	▓		166
5-88	Math Word Search 1			▓	▓	169
5-89	Math Word Search 2			▓	▓	170
5-90	What Doesn't Belong?			▓	▓	171
5-91	Another Kind of Word Search			▓	▓	173
5-92	Creating Sentences with Math Words		▓	▓	▓	175
5-93	Out of This World			▓	▓	177
5-94	Sale Mail			▓	▓	179
5-95	Read All About It!			▓	▓	180
5-96	Is It Really True?			▓	▓	181
5-97	"Reading" a Picture			▓	▓	182
5-98	Where's the Question?			▓	▓	184
5-99	What Am I Looking For?			▓	▓	185
5-100	A Question of Questions			▓	▓	186
5-101	Putting It All Together			▓	▓	188

Chapter 1

HEURISTIC PROBLEMS

Heuristic Problems

What Is a Heuristic Problem?

One objective for mathematics instruction is to enable students to solve problems that:

- represent situations never encountered before,

- have no ready-made algorithm for their solution, and

- require the creation of a unique series of solution steps.

We call these problems "heuristic." Though they are "non-routine" in nature and scope, they are well within the abilities of primary school children to solve.

The term "heuristics" refers to a series of steps and strategies that can be used to solve a problem. These steps do not guarantee the solution: they simply guide the student in the process. George Polya (1945) recommends the following heuristic:

- First, the student must understand the problem and be able to answer the questions:

  What is the question?

  What information is given?

  What are the conditions required by the problem situation?

- Second, the student must find the connection between the information given and the question being asked. The problem solver must devise a solution plan.

- Third, this plan must be carried out.

- Fourth, the solution must be checked.

Problems that require the use of such a general set of steps are called "heuristic problems" in this text. Here is an example of a heuristic problem at the primary level:

Look at the "stairstep numbers" below.
Use your blocks to show the next "stairstep number."

```
                              □
              □         □ □
□           □ □       □ □ □          _____
1           3           6            Number is?
```

Problem solution: The children need to see the pattern of 1, then
1 + 2 = 3, then 1 + 2 + 3 = 6. The pattern can be extended to show
1 + 2 + 3 + 4 = 10. The next "stairstep numeral" is 10.

Instructional Considerations

What may be a heuristic problem to one child may not be for another. In the
above example, a fourth-grade student may grasp the pattern immediately; a
kindergarten student will not.

*Practice with heuristic problems must emphasize the application of
strategies to new or changing problems, not the repetitive application of a
previously created solution pattern.* Children need many experiences in
solving heuristic problems. Their abilities to figure out a problem and create a
solution will improve with experience.

Activity Objectives

The teaching suggestions and activities in this chapter are designed to help
students:

- Identify and apply strategies which can be used with heuristic
  problems in the primary grades. These strategies are taken from the
  following list:

  1. guess and check
  2. eliminate possibilities
  3. make a systematic list
  4. draw or use a picture

  5. look for a pattern
  6. make or use a table
  7. use logical thinking

- Use concrete objects or manipulatives to represent the problem and/or
  act out the problem.

FINGER ADDITION

*H*old up four fingers on each hand. Show children that one group of four and another group of four is eight. Count the fingers on one hand and then the fingers on the other hand to illustrate the fours. Then count all the fingers to show the eight. Write the equation so children can see the numerals and the signs.

4 + 4 = 8

Then ask, "Can you think of another way to show eight with your fingers?"

Discussion:

Have children show their new addends with their fingers. See if they can say the number sentence; help if they can't. Most importantly, watch for the thinking that shows the act of creation or invention of a new idea.

Possible answer:

Variations:

Follow the same steps with the numerals 6, 7, or 9.

Heuristic Problems

CLUES TO THE UNKNOWN

ACTIVITY **2**

Activity One Clue Cards:

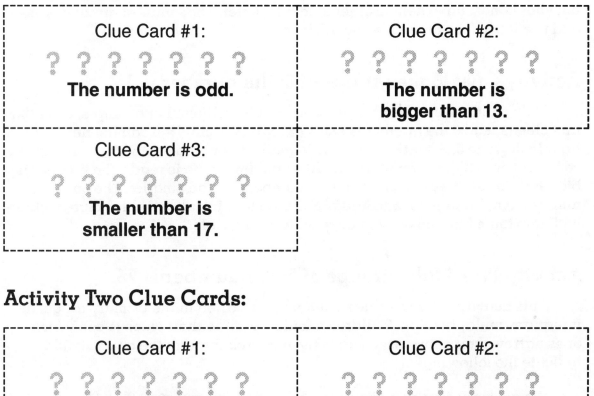

Clue Card #1:

? ? ? ? ? ? ?

The number is odd.

Clue Card #2:

? ? ? ? ? ? ?

The number is bigger than 13.

Clue Card #3:

? ? ? ? ? ? ?

The number is smaller than 17.

Activity Two Clue Cards:

Clue Card #1:

? ? ? ? ? ? ?

The number is a multiple of 3.

Clue Card #2:

? ? ? ? ? ? ?

The number is greater than 8 x 8.

Clue Card #3:

? ? ? ? ? ? ?

The number is an odd number.

Clue Card #4:

? ? ? ? ? ? ?

The number is less than 9 x 9.

Clue Card #5:

? ? ? ? ? ? ?

The sum of the number's digits is an even number.

CLUES TO THE UNKNOWN

ACTIVITY 2

*D*ivide the class into groups of 3 or 4. Cut out each set of "clue cards" on page 15. Tell children they will use these clues to find an unknown number. Only one number should fit all of their clues. Students should read their cards, but should not show them to other students. Later, They must share their clue and use it to check to see if a "possible answer" is a right answer.

Activity One: Make groups of 3; the number is 15.

Help children list possible answers to the problem. For example, after the first clue is read ("the number is smaller than 17"), children can list numerals from 16 down to 0. After the next clue is read ("the number is odd"), children can cross out all the even numbers. After the final clue is read ("the number is bigger than 13") they can cross out all numbers 13 and smaller. The only number remaining is 15. Encourage children to think about which clue or clues will help them find the answer as quickly as possible.

Activity Two: Make groups of 5; the number is 75.

This activity is for the oldest and/or most skilled in the primary range, as it requires multiplication. Children should examine their clues to see which ones narrow their choices most quickly. A search through the clues should indicate the following:

1. We are looking for an odd number that is more than 8 x 8 (64) and less than 9 x 9 (81), so let's list all the odd numbers from 65 to 80.
   65   67   69   71   73   75   77   79

2. Now, which ones are multiples of three? Only the following:
   69   75

3. Which numeral, when you add the digits, gives an even number?
   6 + 9 = 15 Odd   7 + 5 = 12 Even

   The answer is 75.

Suggestion: By using (and varying) similar clues, you can make up additional problems of both types.

Heuristic Problems

SQUARE CHALLENGE

How many squares can you find in each design below? Look carefully or you might be surprised!

Tricky, but not too hard.

1. How many squares can you find in this picture?

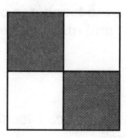

More difficult: Be careful.

2. How many squares can you find in this picture?

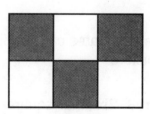

A real challenge!

3. How many squares can you find in this picture?

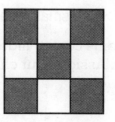

SQUARE CHALLENGE

ACTIVITY **3**

*H*euristic problem-solving activities should be given to all children at all grade levels. The entire act of learning involves inventing solutions for new situations (problems) and trying them out, re-using the ones that work while discarding those that don't. Even learning-disabled children need problem-solving instruction. Consider that one dimension of a learning "disability" may be that children invent and continue to use inadequate or inappropriate solutions to learning/social problems.

The task for the teacher is one of adapting heuristic problems to the children's grade and ability levels. Consider the examples below.

Easiest:

1. How many squares can you find in this picture?

Answer: 5. Four small squares and the entire figure is a square.

Harder:

2. How many squares can you find in this picture?

Answer: 8. Six small squares and then two 4 x 4 squares.

Still More Difficult:

3. How many squares can you find in this picture?

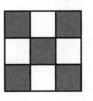

Answer: 14. Nine small, one large, and four 4 x 4 squares.

Note: Problems can be made easier or more difficult by adding squares to the given figure. Assign your children problems that they will find challenging but not frustrating.

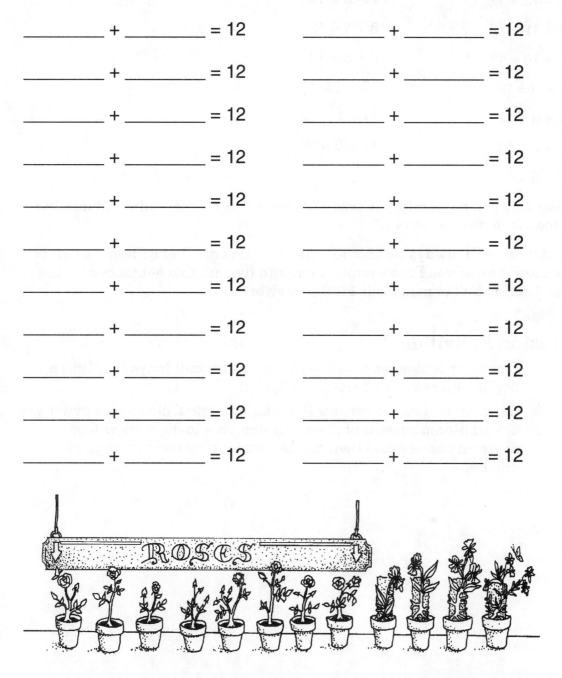

WRITING SENTENCES WITH NUMBERS

How many different number sentences can you write that have 12 as the sum? Remember, you can use only two numerals in each sentence. Use as many of the blank sentences below as you need.

_____ + _____ = 12   _____ + _____ = 12

_____ + _____ = 12   _____ + _____ = 12

_____ + _____ = 12   _____ + _____ = 12

_____ + _____ = 12   _____ + _____ = 12

_____ + _____ = 12   _____ + _____ = 12

_____ + _____ = 12   _____ + _____ = 12

_____ + _____ = 12   _____ + _____ = 12

_____ + _____ = 12   _____ + _____ = 12

_____ + _____ = 12   _____ + _____ = 12

_____ + _____ = 12   _____ + _____ = 12

WRITING SENTENCES WITH NUMBERS

C hildren should find some or all of the following answers. Notice how the use of a pattern makes it easier to find all of the answers.

0 + 12 = 12	7 + 5 = 12
1 + 11 = 12	8 + 4 = 12
2 + 10 = 12	9 + 3 = 12
3 + 9 = 12	10 + 2 = 12
4 + 8 = 12	11 + 1 = 12
5 + 7 = 12	12 + 0 = 12
6 + 6 = 12	

By using only two numerals, you can write a total of thirteen different number sentences with an answer of 12.

Note: You will always be able to write a total of number sentences that is *1* more than the answer. For example, there are five number sentences for the answer 4, nine number sentences for the answer 8.

Expansion Activities:

1. If number sentences equal to 12 are too difficult for your children, begin with smaller numerals (3, 4, or 5).

2. Generating a rule is an excellent mathematical classroom activity. Give children several of these problem sets to do, each with a different answer, and then ask sentences they need for a given number.

From *Primary Problem Solving in Math* by Jack A. Coffland and Gilbert J. Cuevas. Copyright © 1992 by GoodYearBooks.

START YOUR CALCULATORS

ACTIVITY 5

Problem:

How many number sentences using more than two different numerals can you write? (You can't use the same numeral more than once in each sentence, and you can't use zero.)

Examples:

3 + 4 + 5 = 12

1 + 2 + 3 + 6 = 12

Use the lines below for sentences with three numerals.

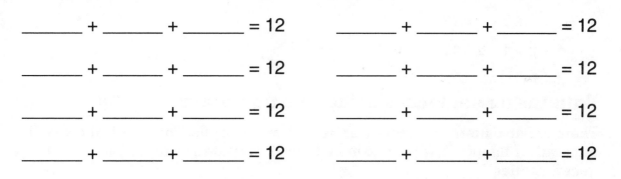

_____ + _____ + _____ = 12   _____ + _____ + _____ = 12

_____ + _____ + _____ = 12   _____ + _____ + _____ = 12

_____ + _____ + _____ = 12   _____ + _____ + _____ = 12

_____ + _____ + _____ = 12   _____ + _____ + _____ = 12

Use the lines below for sentences with four numerals.

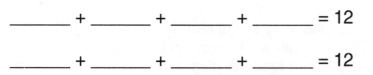

_____ + _____ + _____ + _____ = 12

_____ + _____ + _____ + _____ = 12

Will you need to use this line for a sentence with five numerals?

_____ + _____ + _____ + _____ + _____ = 12

START YOUR CALCULATORS

ACTIVITY 5

*H*and out calculators to the students. Give children time to explore the use of the keys. Briefly go over the use of the + and = keys to add the numerals.

Children should find some or all of the following solutions. Notice how the use of a pattern makes it easier to find all of the answers.

Patterns for sentences using three different numerals:

1 + 2 + 9 = 12	2 + 3 + 7 = 12	3 + 4 + 5 = 12
1 + 3 + 8 = 12	2 + 4 + 6 = 12	
1 + 4 + 7 = 12		
1 + 5 + 6 = 12		

Patterns for sentences using four numerals:

1 + 2 + 3 + 6 = 12

1 + 2 + 4 + 5 = 12

Patterns for sentences using five numerals:

There are no patterns for sentences using five numerals. The smallest possible numerals, 1 through 5, add up to more than 12. Children should try to make this generalization.

1 + 2 + 3 + 4 + 5 = 15

Expansion Activities:

If number sentences equal to 12 are too easy for your children, use slightly larger numerals (13, 14, or 15). This exercise will not provide many possibilities for numerals less than 12, so it is difficult to make it easier.

NAME THAT SHAPE, PART 1

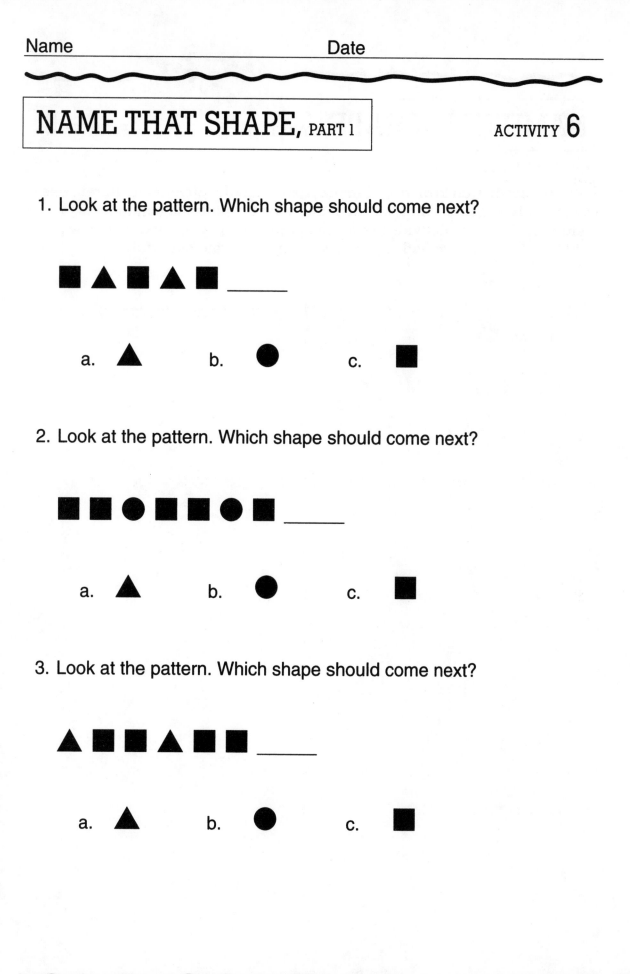

1. Look at the pattern. Which shape should come next?

   ■ ▲ ■ ▲ ■ _____

   a. ▲   b. ●   c. ■

2. Look at the pattern. Which shape should come next?

   ■ ■ ● ■ ■ ● ■ _____

   a. ▲   b. ●   c. ■

3. Look at the pattern. Which shape should come next?

   ▲ ■ ■ ▲ ■ ■ _____

   a. ▲   b. ●   c. ■

NAME THAT SHAPE, PART 1

ACTIVITY 6

Pattern recognition is an excellent heuristic activity for young children. Use manipulatives (blocks, tiles, etc.) to make concrete patterns for students to identify and extend. Activities requiring paper and pencil should be delayed until the children have had experiences using concrete materials.

1. **Answer:** ▲

2. **Answer:** ■

3. **Answer:** ▲

NAME THAT SHAPE, PART 2   ACTIVITY 7

1. Look at the pattern. Do you know what should come next?

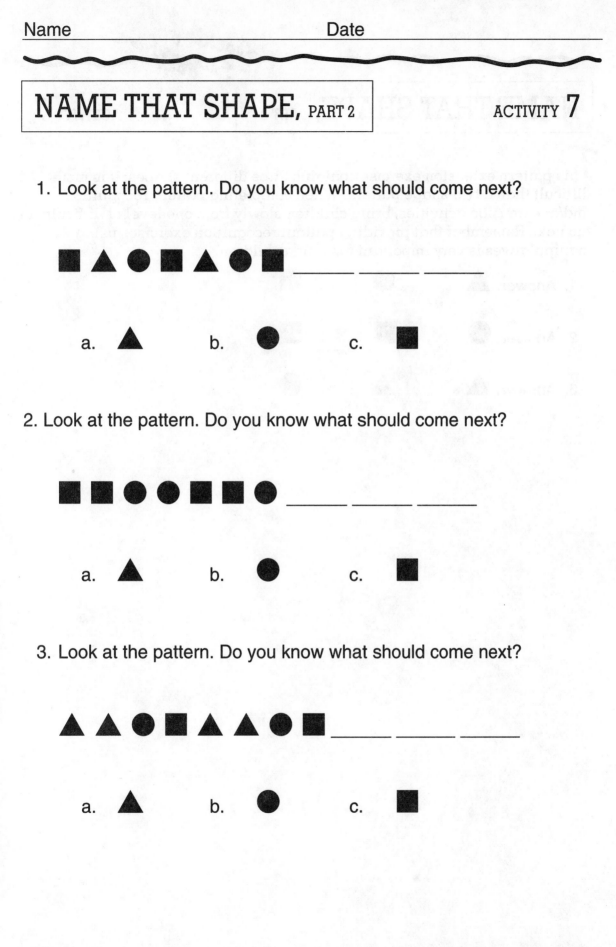

     a. ▲   b. ●   c. ■

2. Look at the pattern. Do you know what should come next?

     a. ▲   b. ●   c. ■

3. Look at the pattern. Do you know what should come next?

     a. ▲   b. ●   c. ■

From *Primary Problem Solving in Math* by Jack A. Coffland and Gilbert J. Cuevas. Copyright © 1992 by GoodYearBooks.

NAME THAT SHAPE, PART 2

ACTIVITY 7

This pattern extension exercise contains three different shapes; it is more difficult than a two-shape pattern. When completing pattern recognition and/or extension activities, bring children slowly from one level of difficulty to the next. Remember that providing pattern recognition exercises using manipulatives is very important for young children.

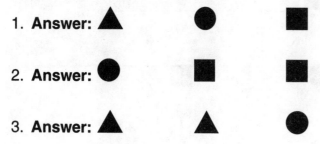

1. **Answer:** ▲ ● ■

2. **Answer:** ● ■ ■

3. **Answer:** ▲ ▲ ●

WHAT COMES NEXT?

Circle the picture that should come next.

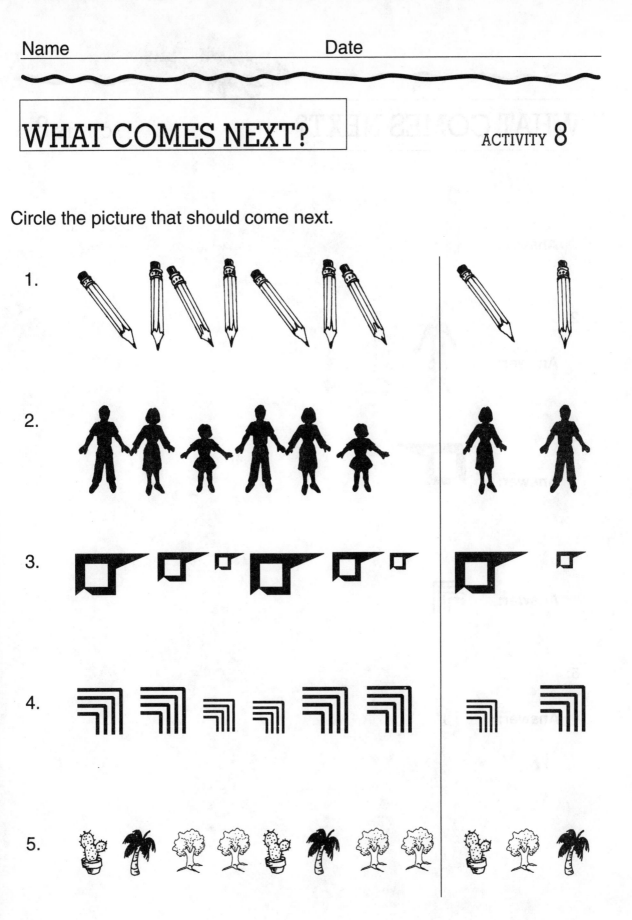

WHAT COMES NEXT?

ACTIVITY 8

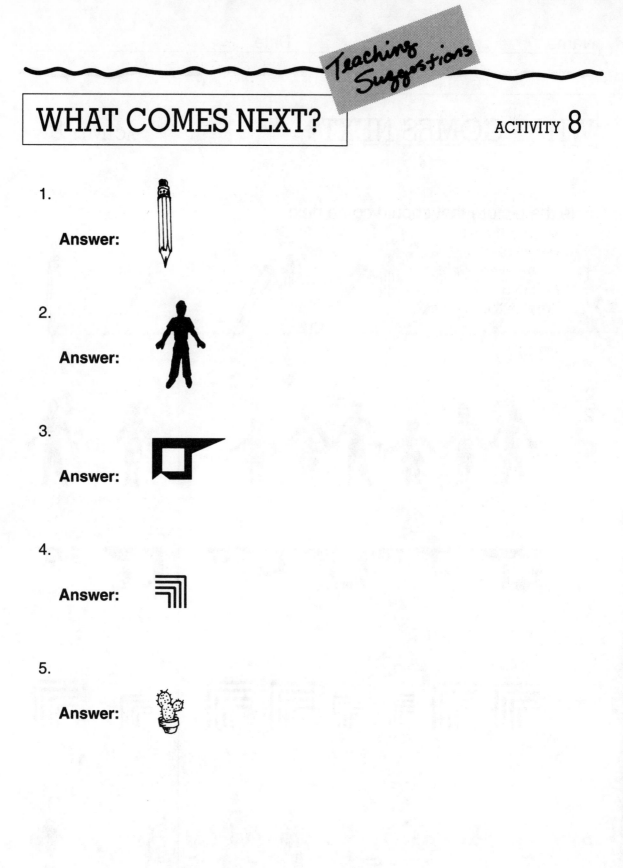

1.

Answer:

2.

Answer:

3.

Answer:

4.

Answer:

5.

Answer:

MYSTERY NUMBERS

1. I am thinking of a mystery number. Can you use these clues to discover what the mystery number is?   It is
   - ■ less than 10
   - ■ bigger than 5
   - ■ an even number
   - ■ not 8

   What is the number? _____

Guess	Check	Reason
7	Wrong	It is not an even number.
8		
6		

   What is the mystery number?_____

2. Let's figure out another mystery number. Use these clues to discover what it is. It is
   - ■ less than 10
   - ■ not 9
   - ■ bigger than 5
   - ■ an odd number

Guess	Check	Reason

   What is the mystery number?_____

3. I will give you the clues for the next mystery number. Write them below

Guess	Check	Reason

   What is the mystery number?_____

Heuristic Problems

MYSTERY NUMBERS

ACTIVITY 9

*H*aving students guess the answer to a problem and then comparing it with the actual answer is an important mathematical strategy. It provides a means for encouraging students to *estimate* the answer to a word problem and then to check the *feasibility* of that estimate. Problems 1 and 2 are examples of heuristic problems that can be solved using the "guess and check" strategy.

1. You may wish to help students develop a chart like the one below to record their "guesses" and "checks":

Guess	Check	Reason
7	Wrong	It is not an even number.
8	Wrong	Number is not 8.
6	Right	Is even, is less than 10 and is greater than 5.

The mystery number is 6.

2.

Guess	Check	Reason
6	Wrong	It is not an odd number.
8	Wrong	It is not an odd number.
9	Wrong	Number is not 9.
7	Right	Is odd, is less than 10 and is greater than 5.

The mystery number is 7.

3. In creating your own problems, use the clues that relate to the math you are teaching. For example, if you are teaching addition, then:

    1. The number is smaller than 10.

    2. It is bigger than 5.

    3. It is equal to 4 + 3.

FUN WITH BEADS

ACTIVITY 10

Suzie needs four more beads for her necklace. Can you find the beads she needs at the bottom of the page? Cut them out and place them here. Remember to use the same pattern that Suzie started.

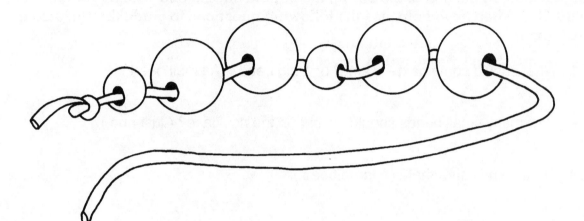

From *Primary Problem Solving in Math* by Jack A. Coffland and Gilbert J. Cuevas. Copyright © 1992 by GoodYearBooks.

31

FUN WITH BEADS

Mathematics has been described as the science of patterns. Having young children find patterns is always an excellent mathematical activity.

The pattern on this worksheet consists of one small bead followed by two large beads. At the end of the string, the pattern should end with one small bead. If children need help, use the following questions to guide the classroom discussion:

1. What should come next—a small or a big bead? (A small bead.)

2. How many small beads should we put on the necklace? (Just one.)

3. What comes after that? (A large bead.)

4. How many? (Two.)

5. How many beads have we put on the necklace? (Three.)

6. How many are we supposed to put on? (Four.)

7. We need one more. What should it be? (A small bead.)

8. Now let's check. Do we have the same pattern, all the way across the necklace?

You may want to present this activity with manipulatives. If so, make a necklace out of "pop beads" or beads on a string. Provide the children with additional beads to use while completing the necklace.

For younger children, restrict the necklace pattern to one attribute (shape, color, or size). For example, keep the pop beads or string beads all the same size, varying only the color. For more mature children, you might want to try patterns involving both size and color.

From *Primary Problem Solving in Math* by Jack A. Coffland and Gilbert J. Cuevas. Copyright © 1992 by GoodYearBooks.

Heuristic Problems

THINKING OF EVERYTHING! ACTIVITY 11

1. What is the least amount of money you could spend at this sale?

2. What is the most amount of money you could spend at this sale?

3. List all the possible combinations of things you could buy at this sale. How much money would each one cost?

4. Now look at your list. What amounts of money can't you spend at the sale?

What Is Purchased?	Amount Spent (¢)

THINKING OF EVERYTHING!

ACTIVITY 11

G uide children in listing all the combinations of items that can be bought. Help them include the corresponding money amounts. If students are having trouble, discuss the following points with them:

- ■ I could spend nothing at the sale. The minimum I could spend is 0 cents.

- ■ Or, I could buy up to three of each of the items. That would be 6 cents for the pencils and 9 cents for the erasers. The maximum amount I could spend is 15 cents.

What Is Purchased?	Amount Spent (¢)
Nothing	0¢
1 pencil	2¢
1 eraser	3¢
2 pencils	4¢
1 pencil, 1 eraser	5¢
2 erasers or 3 pencils	6¢
2 pencils, 1 eraser	7¢
2 erasers, 1 pencil	8¢
3 erasers, or 3 pencils/1 eraser	9¢
2 erasers, 2 pencils	10¢
3 erasers, 1 pencil	11¢
3 pencils, 2 erasers	12¢
3 erasers, 2 pencils	13¢
3 erasers, 3 pencils	15¢

Note: You cannot spend 1¢ or 14¢ at this sale.

Problem source: Wirtz, Robert. Speech at National Council of Teachers of Mathematics Conference, Seattle, Washington, 1980.

THE FIVE LITTLE PIGS GO HOME

The Story of the Five Little Pigs

▷ Five little pigs came home from the market. The first one went to his blue house. The second one went to his green house. The third and fourth pigs lived together. They went to their yellow house. The big bad wolf blew the fifth pig's house away. So, this little pig went to a house that was not blue and that only one pig lived in.

Color each of the houses. Use the story to tell you which colors to use. Then cut out the pigs and place them in the house where each one belongs.

From *Primary Problem Solving in Math* by Jack A. Coffland and Gilbert J. Cuevas. Copyright © 1992 by GoodYearBooks.

THE FIVE LITTLE PIGS GO HOME

ACTIVITY 12

The teaching strategy underlying this problem is central to mathematics instruction. Here children use manipulatives in solving the problem of where the fifth little pig lives. Manipulatives give students an opportunity to visualize and/or experience the problem. Whenever possible and as frequently as possible, have students use concrete or manipulative objects to represent and solve problems. A variety of manipulative materials should always be available for students to use with problem-solving activities.

Extension:

You may also wish to use objects to represent the houses and the pigs and have children act out the problem. Similar "direction following" problems help children represent and solve problems. They provide excellent experiences for acting out the words that are being read.

BUILDING A TEN

Can you find four whole numbers that add up to 10? You may not use a number more than once. Cut out the ten squares at the bottom of the page and arrange the ones you want in the boxes. How many different answers can you find?

BUILDING A TEN

*T*o guide students' thinking, you may wish to use the following approach:

"In this problem we need to find four different numbers that add up to 10. Are there any that you already know won't work?" Write down ideas on the board which seem to limit the possible answers. Ask students to support their strategies. The following is an example:

Teacher: Why can't we use many big numbers?

Student: Because 10 + 9 is 19. That's already too big.

Teacher: Excellent. So what should we use?

Student: We probably have to use little numbers.

Teacher: Can you give me examples?

Student: Well, 1 + 2 + 3 = 6. What number plus 6 equals 10? It's 4.

Teacher: So, now we have one answer. 1 + 2 + 3 + 4 = 10.   Are there any other possible answers?

Student: I don't think so. We've used the four smallest numbers. If we make any of them bigger, our answer will be too big.

A strategy like this helps narrow down the things that have to be checked. It also requires children to put abstract ideas into words.

Answer: If zero is not used, 1 + 2 + 3 + 4 = 10 is the only answer.

If zero is used, the following combinations are also possible:

a. 0 + 1 + 2 + 7 = 10   c. 0 + 1 + 4 + 5 = 10

b. 0 + 1 + 3 + 6 = 10   d. 0 + 2 + 3 + 5 = 10

Variations:

1. Have smaller children put manipulatives in the boxes. It will be easier for them to move concrete objects.

2. Do the problem allowing numbers to be used more than once. Given this situation, there are many possible answers.

Note: Developing math ideas with more than one correct answer is always a good idea.

From *Primary Problem Solving in Math* by Jack A. Coffland and Gilbert J. Cuevas. Copyright © 1992 by GoodYearBooks.

COIN COUNTDOWN

▷ Mary and Peter were counting
the coins they found under a bridge. Mary was very careful. While she counted 2 coins, Peter counted 3. Together they counted 15 coins. How many coins did each child count?

Find the answer to this problem. Making a chart or table might help.

From *Primary Problem Solving in Math* by Jack A. Coffland and Gilbert J. Cuevas. Copyright © 1992 by GoodYearBooks.

COIN COUNTDOWN

T ables can help children organize the information presented in a problem, thus giving them a logical view of the data being considered. Tables can also assist in visualizing all of the possible outcomes a problem may have. With small children, you may wish to give them a table they can use to solve a problem. Older children may create their own.

Consider this problem, which can be solved by using a table.

Mary and Peter were counting the coins they found under a bridge. Mary was very careful. While she counted 2 coins, Peter counted 3. Together they counted 15 coins. How many coins did each child count?

Find the answer to this problem.

To get children started, discuss what the table would show. Be sure the following ideas are identified:

a. The coins counted by the careful child (Mary).

b. The coins counted by the fast child (Peter).

c. The total number of coins counted.

	Number of coins counted by:			
Mary	2	4	6	8
Peter	3	6	9	12
Total Coins Counted:	5	10	15	20

Heuristic Problems

CALCULATOR CAPERS

ACTIVITY 15

1. Maria spent 25¢ at the school store. She bought two things. What did she buy?

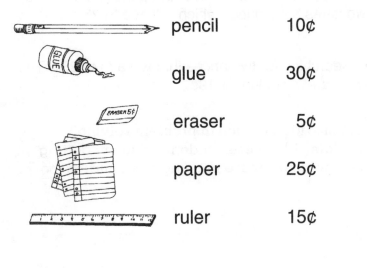

pencil	10¢
glue	30¢
eraser	5¢
paper	25¢
ruler	15¢

_____ ¢ plus _____ ¢ = _____ ¢

2. Mike bought two items at the school cafeteria. He spent 25¢ for dessert. Which two foods did Mike buy?

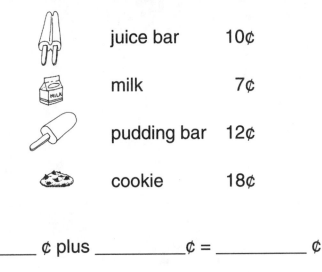

juice bar	10¢
milk	7¢
pudding bar	12¢
cookie	18¢

_____ ¢ plus _____ ¢ = _____ ¢

From *Primary Problem Solving in Math* by Jack A. Coffland and Gilbert J. Cuevas. Copyright © 1992 by GoodYearBooks.

CALCULATOR CAPERS

ACTIVITY 15

*D*irections: Pair the students. Give each pair a calculator.

1. **Answer:** Maria bought two items. The student must examine the prices and select the only two items whose prices will sum to 25¢: the pencil for 10¢ and the ruler for 15¢. No other two items have prices which will add to 25¢.

2. **Answer:** Again, students are searching for two prices that will add to 25¢. The only possibilities are: milk for 7¢ and a cookie for 18¢.

Computational drill does not provide practice in problem solving. However, in solving heuristic problems like these, students also are getting practice in computation. Here they get experience in using a calculator, too.

From *Primary Problem Solving in Math* by Jack A. Coffland and Gilbert J. Cuevas. Copyright © 1992 by GoodYearBooks.

TRIANGLE PUZZLE

 How many triangles can you find in this figure?

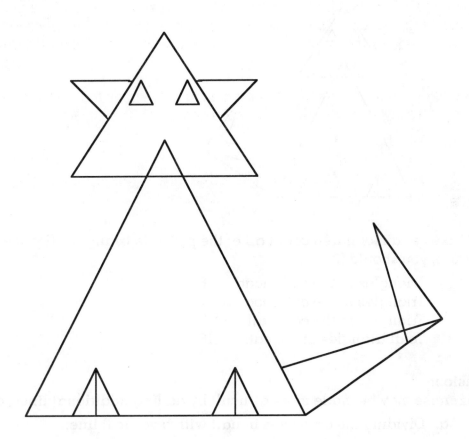

From *Primary Problem Solving in Math* by Jack A. Coffland and Gilbert J. Cuevas. Copyright © 1992 by GoodYearBooks.

TRIANGLE PUZZLE

How many triangles can you find in this figure?

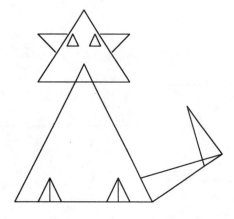

Make certain children count all of the possible triangles. If you examine the figure, you should find:

Triangles in the cat's head = 6
Triangles in the cat's body = 7
Triangles in the cat's tail = 3
Total triangles in the cat: 16

Extension:

The exercise may be made more difficult by adding additional lines, as:

a. Dividing the cat's eyes in half with a vertical line.

b. Adding another triangle to the tail.

c. Dividing the cat's feet into thirds by using two lines in each foot rather than one.

Problem modified from: Spitzer, Herbert F. *Practical Classroom Procedures for Enriching Arithmetic.* St. Louis, MO: Webster Publishing Company, 1956.

VALUABLE SHAPES, PART 1   ACTIVITY 17

These shapes are worth money. A ▲ = 4 cents, a ● = 8 cents, and a ■ = 15 cents.

How much are they worth when you put them together?

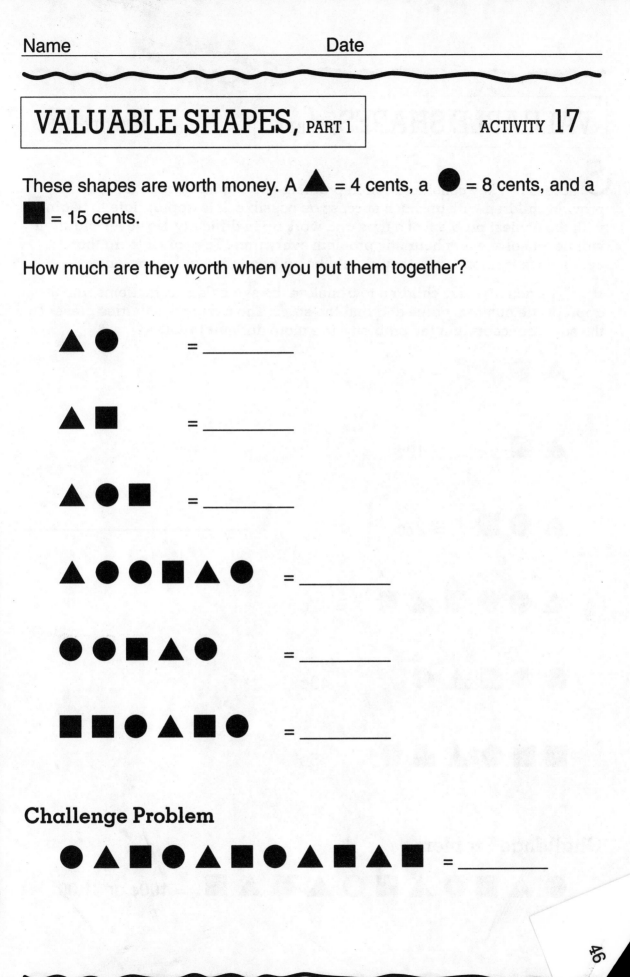

▲● = _____

▲■ = _____

▲●■ = _____

▲●●■▲● = _____

●●■▲● = _____

■■■●▲■● = _____

Challenge Problem

●■▲■●▲■●▲■▲■ = _____

Heuristic P.

VALUABLE SHAPES, PART 1

Success is a key consideration in problem-solving instruction. In order to provide children with as much success as possible, it is appropriate to begin with the easiest problem of a type and work up in difficulty. However, children will never solve every heuristic problem every time. They must learn that persistence is important—they should be willing to try and try again.

This activity asks children to translate the symbols or code items into the appropriate numeral value and find the sums. The next two activities present the same concepts, but the problems are more difficult to solve.

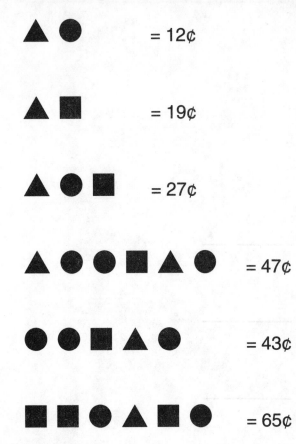

▲ ● = 12¢

▲ ■ = 19¢

▲ ● ■ = 27¢

▲ ● ● ■ ▲ ● = 47¢

● ● ■ ▲ ● = 43¢

■ ■ ● ▲ ■ ● = 65¢

Challenge Problem

● ▲ ■ ● ▲ ■ ● ▲ ■ ▲ ■ = 100¢ or $1.00

From *Primary Problem Solving in Math* by Jack A. Coffland and Gilbert J. Cuevas. Copyright © 1992 by GoodYearBooks.

Name _____   Date _____

VALUABLE SHAPES, PART 2   ACTIVITY 18

These shapes are worth money. A ▲ = 4 cents, and and a ■ = 15 cents.

Use this information to find out what the ● is worth in each of the problems below.

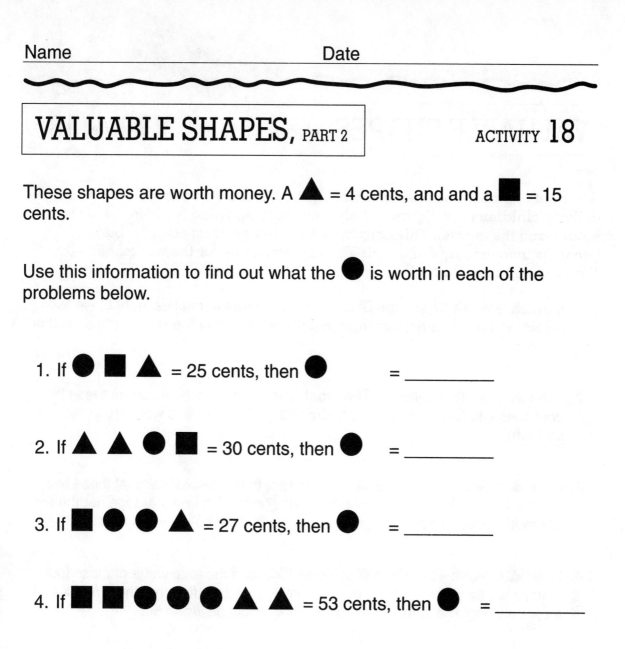

1. If ● ■ ▲ = 25 cents, then ●   = _____

2. If ▲ ▲ ● ■ = 30 cents, then ●   = _____

3. If ■ ● ● ▲ = 27 cents, then ●   = _____

4. If ■ ■ ● ● ● ▲ ▲ = 53 cents, then ●   = _____

VALUABLE SHAPES, PART 2 ACTIVITY 18

This set of problems presents a more difficult code value exercise. For this activity, children must figure out what the missing value is given the other values and the answer. This activity is structured so that each problem becomes increasingly difficult. It also is preparation for the worksheet "Valuable Shapes, Part 3."

1. If the ▲ is worth 4¢ and the ■ is worth 15¢, then the total value of these two objects is 19¢. Subtract that from 25¢ and we find that the ● is worth 6¢ in this problem.

2. If the ▲ is worth 4¢ and the ■ is worth 15¢, then the total value for these three objects is 23¢. Subtract that from 30¢ and we find the ● is worth 7¢ in this problem.

3. If the ▲ is worth 4¢ and the ■ is worth 15¢, then the total value of these two objects is 19¢. Subtract this amount from 27¢ and we find that together the two ●s must be worth 8¢ in this problem. Each ● must be worth 4¢ here.

4. If the ▲ is worth 4¢ and the ■ is worth 15¢, then the total value of these four objects is 38¢. Subtract this amount from 53¢ and we find that the three ●s must be worth 15¢ in this problem. Each ● must be worth 5¢.

From *Primary Problem Solving in Math* by Jack A. Coffland and Gilbert J. Cuevas. Copyright © 1992 by GoodYearBooks.

VALUABLE SHAPES, PART 3

The following shapes are worth money. A ▲ = 4 cents, a ● = 8 cents, and a ■ = 15 cents. What shapes would you need to put together in order to total each of the amounts below?

a. 23 cents   =

b. 20 cents   =

c. 38 cents   =

d. 27 cents   =

e. 50 cents   =

f. 66 cents   =

g. 29 cents   =

VALUABLE SHAPES, PART 3

ACTIVITY 19

This is the most difficult "code value" activity. Children must be able to use the codes to represent different amounts. *Possible* solutions are shown below. Note that the last problem may be especially difficult for children, but they should get used to proving to themselves that a problem has no possible answer.

a. 23 cents = ● ■ or ▲ ▲ ■

b. 20 cents = ▲ ▲ ▲ ▲ ▲ or ▲ ● ●

c. 38 cents = ● ■ ■ or ▲ ▲ ■ ■

d. 27 cents = ▲ ● ■ or ▲ ▲ ▲ ■

e. 50 cents = ▲ ● ● ■ ■ or ▲ ▲ ▲ ▲ ▲ ■ ■

f. 66 cents = ▲ ● ● ● ● ■ ■ or

▲ ▲ ▲ ▲ ▲ ▲ ▲ ▲ ▲ ■ ■

g. 29 cents = Cannot be made from the values given.

BUILDING A TOY

ACTIVITY **20**

▷ Here are some shapes you can use to build your own toy. Cut out the shapes you want and build your toy on another piece of paper. You must buy the shapes you use. After you are done, figure the cost of your toy.

Shapes

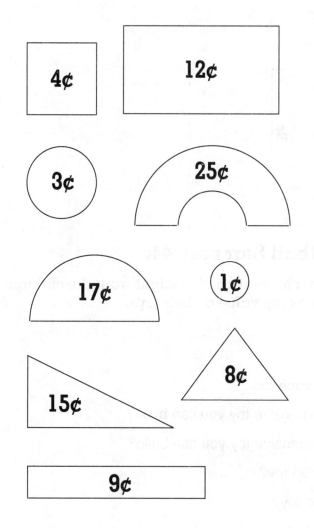

BUILDING A TOY

ACTIVITY **20**

An Example: Benito the Basketball Star

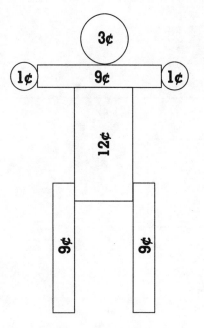

Benito the Basketball Star cost: 44¢

Answers will vary for each question. You might want the children to use a calculator to add or check the value of their toys.

Enrichment:

Follow with questions such as:

What is the most expensive toy you can build?

What is the least expensive toy you can build?

Can you build a $1.00 toy?

Can you build a 50¢ toy?

Create your own shapes, give each a price, and copy them onto colored paper. Ask children to use them in creating pictures of their choice. Have them find the value for their pictures.

SITUATIONAL PROBLEMS

Situational Problems

$\mathcal{S}$ ituational problems are drawn from real-life experiences. They are multiple-step problems that require students to consider a wide variety of variables related to the outcome. To solve a situational problem, students must:

- identify factors related to the solution,

- include these factors in the plan for solving the problem,

- make the necessary computations, and,

- arrive at a solution based upon the combination of thinking and calculating.

Situational problems are open-ended in nature, so all students will not arrive at the same solution. For example:

> There are six people waiting for a snack. There are only three cupcakes. What should we do?

Children's suggestions will vary. However, you may want to guide the group toward a solution that is fair to all and that also provides a snack for everyone.

Instructional Considerations

Situational problems need to be discussed and solved by the whole class or cooperative learning groups. Situational problems *introduce* the skills needed to deal with non-routine problems. They are designed9to acquaint students with the "process-oriented" nature of problem solving.

Problem solving is a complex process involving a variety of skills. These skills include:
- reading
- logical thinking
- use of problem-solving strategies
- computational skills
- the ability to use *previous knowledge and experiences* to relate the problem to meaningful context
- the appropriate use of *technological tools* such as calculators and computers

- a representation of the problem through the use of *concrete materials*
- the ability to work in *cooperative learning groups* and to learn from the efforts of everyone in the group

As they build these skills, students also develop the motivation to "stick" with a problem, even when the solution is not immediately evident. Many times students express comments such as:

- "It's too hard." Perhaps what is really meant is: "A problem I can't solve in ten seconds is not worth the effort."

- "Don't tell me how to do it, just tell me I'm right." Perhaps what is meant here is: "This problem IS too hard and I don't have *any* idea how to solve it!" or "I've guessed an operation, worked a problem, and all you have to do is tell me if it's correct. If not, I'll guess another operation and be back in 30 seconds. I definitely won't think about problem solving."

- "I don't get this one." A possible message: "I've read this one through (maybe), the operation was not obvious, and now I want you to tell me how to do it."

To learn the true nature of problem solving, children should solve problems that are non-routine, meaningful, interesting, challenging, and multi-step. Children need to see that we all solve "problems" every day of our lives. They should be involved with other students in solving interesting problems. Input from the teacher is important, too, in showing how experience may help in suggesting things to consider. Situational problems provide these kinds of opportunities for children.

Activity Objectives

This chapter deals with suggested procedures and activities to involve students actively in solving situational problems. The students will:

1. Assume a role in a problem-solving group.
2. Use a calculator, when necessary, to do problem computations.
3. Identify and list key factors related to the problem.
4. Identify strategies or approaches for answering the question posed in the problem.
5. Verbalize the solution to the problem.

The activities in this chapter are presented in two formats: Problems for young children that emphasize classroom discussions and the use of a blackboard or bulletin board; and problems presented on reproducible pages for distribution to a small group or the entire class.

DISCUSSION ACTIVITIES

Young children can't read and write well enough to solve many situational problems with pencil and paper. For kindergarten or first-grade students, situational problems are usually presented as "discussion problems." Consider using the following problem situations as small-group or whole-class activities. These activities are designed to help children see that problem solving is a process that requires exploration and communication, and one in which answers are not always readily obtained.

ACTIVITY 21

Classroom routines may suggest excellent discussion problems for young children. Almost every kindergarten class has "snack time." How can snack time be used for situational problem solving?

Situation: The Cupcake Dilemma

Seat 6 children at a table and present this problem:

"It's time for these 6 children to have a snack. But I only have 3 cupcakes. What can I do?"

Lead children in discussing possible ways to solve the problem. Children's responses may range from:

"Let's not have a snack today." to "Give them to three of us; the others don't get a snack."

Direct children's thinking towards a solution with questions such as:

"Do you really want to miss the snack today?" or

"Do you think it is fair to just let three children have a snack?"

The obvious solution is for the children to cut the cupcakes in half. If the students arrive at another solution they all agree upon and is fair to everyone, accept it.

Expand the problem using 5 cupcakes to see if children can transfer what they have learned to a similar problem with a different quantity. (Don't be surprised, however, if children choose to divide 3 cupcakes, leaving the other 2 untouched.)

G iving accurate and precise directions can be a problem for many young children. Consider the following problem which asks children to be precise in the use of language when giving directions.

Situation: The Peanut Butter Sandwich

Have children gather their chairs around a table. On the table is a loaf of bread, a jar of peanut butter, a table knife, and a jar of jam. Then state:

"Children, I've just arrived from the planet Mars. I've heard that here on Earth you have a wonderful thing called a peanut butter sandwich. I was told to buy the things on this table, but now, I don't know how to make the sandwich. Can you give me directions?"

The point of this exercise is to have children tell you *exactly* what to do. The teacher's job is to deliberately misunderstand incomplete or inaccurate directions. For example:

To begin, children might say: "Teacher, take the peanut butter and jam and put it on the bread." Your response: Move the jars of peanut butter and jam and set them on top of the loaf of bread.

To discuss spreading the peanut butter, children might say: "Put the peanut butter on the bread." Your response: Take a knife covered with peanut butter and place it on the bread.

To get tme peanut butter out of the jar, children might say: "Put the knife in the peanut butter." Your response: Put the knife into the peanut butter and leave it.

In this manner, guide the children to communicate the exact actions necessary to make a peanut butter sandwich. Consider each suggestion carefully. Take literally what the children are saying. Ask the children to refine their directions until they see that the physical actions match the verbal instructions.

Note: When this activity was done in a kindergarten class, it took over 30 minutes to finish. At the end, 20 hungry children looked at a teacher holding a piece of bread covered with peanut butter in her left hand and a piece of bread covered with jam in her right hand. They didn't know how to finish the task. Finally, one child blurted out, "Teacher, just clap!" They cheered as she did and the sandwich was finally completed.

Teaching Suggestions

Making lists can be integrated into problem-solving activities. Consider the following:

Situation: Vegetable Soup

Plan to make a vegetable soup in class. Introduce the activity by saying:

"Let's make a vegetable soup for our snack tomorrow. What would you like to have in our soup?"

Ask children to list the ingredients that might be put into the soup. (We are assuming that the children know what vegetables are. If this is not the case, you may wish to conduct some preparatory lessons on the topic.)

Some of the children may respond to an item on the list as follows: "I don't like carrots." or "I won't eat broccoli." At this point, discuss what to do. For example:

"We have a problem. Janis likes carrots, but Billy doesn't. What can we do?"

Solicit suggestions from the children. Try to get them to identify ways in which the class can agree on the ingredients. Some strategies to consider include:

a. Listing all the possible ingredients on the board, and then voting on what should be included.

b. Not listing some vegetables because they are disliked by almost everyone.

c. Including all vegetables with the understanding that children only have to eat what they like.

d. If children don't want vegetable soup, ask them to decide what they would like instead. Here, however, emphasize that the goal is to make something with vegetables, not something like chili or peanut butter sandwiches. Guide children to focus on the reasons for making soup (e.g., "We are making vegetable soup to study different food groups. We can't make chili because it does not contain many different vegetabler.").

The best solution would be a decision to make a soup that everyone can eat for a snack, even if all the children don't like everything in the soup.

Conflicts in classroom routines may also present a situational or "discussion" problem for children. For example:

Situation: Just One Computer

Share your observation with children that the class computer seems to be causing some problems. There are disagreements about who gets to use it. Ask, "With _____ children and only one computer, can we think of a way that everyone can use it—a way that is fair to everyone?"

Focus the discussion on two key points:

■ everyone needs time on the computer, and

■ the class can make up rules which are fair and which do not cause problems.

Situational problems emphasize multiple possibilities for discussion. They also require that more than one point of view be considered. For example, you and your class may decide to list all the suggestions and vote on which ones to try. Or, you may experiment with one suggestion for a week and then try another suggestion the next week.

Structure similar problems based on other classroom routines.

Using accurate information is an excellent skill to teach young children. When presented with a problem, children often make wild, inaccurate guesses. Children need opportunities to experiment with quantities and to consider how accurate these numbers describe real-life situations. Consider the following:

Situation: Getting Ready for School

"What time should I get up so I can get to school on time?"

In discussing this question, the objective is to get children to *list* all the things they have to do before school, and to figure out how long they take. This may be a problem, as young children may have difficulty estimating time.

Responses may range from: "I eat breakfast in one minute." to "I have to get dressed. That takes 40 minutes."

One way to remedy this lack of skills is to have children list everything they have to do to get ready for school first. Send home the list and ask parents to help the children record the time it takes them to do each activity.

The objective of the exercise is not only to list everything which needs to be considered to solve the problem, but also to collect information about the length of time each activity takes. Stress this aspect of the problem. Talk about the process of data collecting and how scientists use numbers to answer questions.

ACTIVITY 26

*P*roblems in the community might be used as situational problems in the kindergarten or first-grade classroom. For example:

Situation: Not Enough Water

"Children, we're having a water shortage in our community. How can we save water here at school?"

Note: You may want to discuss with the children beforehand what a water shortage is and the problems it creates.

List the ways that water is used at school. Then explore children's ideas for how water might be saved.

ACTIVITY 27

*C*lassroom pets suggest many excellent activities, from teaching children how to be responsible for the care of a pet to the mathematics of how much it costs to keep the pet.

Situation: A Classroom Pet

"It would be nice if we could have a pet for our classroom. What kind would you like? We also should consider how much effort it would take to care for the pets we are thinking about."

Make a table like the one below that shows the possible pets you might

From *Primary Problem Solving in Math* by Jack A. Coffland and Gilbert J. Cuevas. Copyright © 1992 by GoodYearBooks.

Situational Problems

have in a classroom (fish, hamster, mice, etc.) Discuss and
list what the children would have to do to take care of each pet. Also discuss
how much it would cost to keep each pet suggested. Guide children as they
work toward a decision. Emphasize the criteria for selection (i.e, cheapest,
least trouble to keep, etc).

Pet	What we need to take care of the pet	How much will it cost?
Dog		

ACTIVITY **28**

Field trips offer still more possibilities for situational problems.

Situation: Our Field Trip to the Zoo

"Class, we're going to take a field trip to the zoo next Tuesday. We will need to
plan. What should we take with us to the zoo?"

Make a list of all items suggested (lunches, cold drinks in an ice chest, paper
and pencil to record what we see, coats if it is cold, baseball and bat to play
during lunch, etc.). Discuss why each item suggested may or may not be
needed. Make a final list for each student.

ACTIVITY **29**

Classroom parties provide many possibilities for situational problems. In
addition, this is a good opportunity to show students the use of a calculator.
For example:

Situation: Our Valentine's Party

"Children, we have $20 in our party fund to spend on our Valentine's Day Party.
How should we spend it?"

List children's suggestions on the board. There are several ways to obtain the
cost of each item. Consider the following steps:

    a. Take a field trip to a store and find the prices for all items on the
       list.

    b. Use newspaper advertisements to find prices.

c.   The teacher may play the role of the cash register. Example: when soda is suggested, write: "30¢ for 1 can of soda." How many can do we need? How much will that cost? Or, when cupcakes are suggested, either give the price of a package of cupcakes at the store or reasonable costs for the ingredients. Then have the class total what the cupcakes will cost.

When all prices have been obtained, have the children decide on how to spend their $20. Seek consensus through discussion, voting, or other such methods.

ACTIVITY 30

Sharing classroom toys also presents excellent activities with multiple-solution possibilities. Consider the following:

Situation: Sharing Blocks

"Two children want to play with our blocks. We only have 30 blocks. What should we do?"

Discuss possibilities. Taking turns and dividing the blocks obviously are two of the strategies students may use. List the possibilities on the board. Have children decide which would be the best ones.

Extension:
The problem can be made more difficult with a larger number of children and with a number of blocks that does not divide evenly.

ACTIVITY 31

A Bagful of Problems
   1.   Lisa is making a snack for her three friends. She is going to give them milk and cookies. Tell me everything she has to do to fix the snack.
   2.   Jimmy is having a party. It will last 30 minutes. What games should he play?
   3.   We are going to the beach Saturday. What should we take with us?
   4.   We have 3 hours of class before lunch. We need to do reading, math, spelling, and science. How should we arrange our morning?

From *Primary Problem Solving in Math* by Jack A. Coffland and Gilbert J. Cuevas. Copyright © 1992 by GoodYearBooks.

5. We are going to have a school field day. What games should we play? How do we divide the class into teams?

6. What supplies does each student need to have for school? How much will they cost?

PLANNING A FIELD TRIP ACTIVITY 32

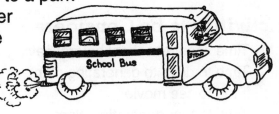 Our class will take a field trip to see how electricity is produced. First we will tour an electrical plant and then we will see a movie and a demonstration. Next we will go to a park for a picnic and a baseball game. After lunch we will visit a dam. Do we have time to take this trip during the school day?

1. What we want to do:

   _____   _____

   _____   _____

   _____   _____

2. How much time will each activity take?

   Activity: Time:

   _____   _____

   _____   _____

   _____   _____

   _____   _____

   _____   _____

   _____   _____

3. Can we take this trip in one day?

   _____ Yes. It will be a great day!

   _____ No. What activities should we cut out?

From *Primary Problem Solving in Math* by Jack A. Coffland and Gilbert J. Cuevas. Copyright © 1992 by GoodYearBooks.

PLANNING A FIELD TRIP

ACTIVITY **32**

The following are suggested activities and the approximate time each activity might take.

Activities to be Considered

Time spent at school before leaving
Time to drive to generating plant
Time to see movie
Time to tour generating plant
Time to drive to dam
Time to tour dam
Time for picnic lunch
Time to drive back to school
Time spent at school before leaving for home

Suggested Time For Each Activity

Time is spent at school before leaving	10 minutes
Time to drive to generating plant	30 minutes
Time to see movie	30 minutes
Time to tour generating plant	35 minutes
Time to drive to picnic	40 minutes
Time for picnic	30 minutes
Time for the baseball game	45 minutes
Time to drive to dam	15 minutes
Time to tour dam	30 minutes
Time to drive back to school	5 minutes
Time spent at school to end of day	10 minutes
Total time	5 hours 50 minutes
How long does school last?	5 hours 30 minutes

Can we take this trip?

Answers will obviously vary. Help children see that what they would like to do is not always the same as what they can do, and choices have to be made accordingly.

From *Primary Problem Solving in Math* by Jack A. Coffland and Gilbert J. Cuevas. Copyright © 1992 by GoodYearBooks.

Situational Problems

SCOUTING OUTING

ACTIVITY **33**

▷ Your Brownie troop is planning a camping trip. Each Brownie needs to take money to pay for:

  supper at a fast food restaurant
  transportation
  admission to a state park
  activities at the park

If you get $10, will you have enough money for the trip?

1. What do you need money for?

  _____   _____

  _____   _____

  _____   _____

2. What are the costs?

  Activity: Time:

  _____   _____

  _____   _____

  _____   _____

  _____   _____

  _____   _____

  _____   _____

3. Can you afford to take this trip?

From *Primary Problem Solving in Math* by Jack A. Coffland and Gilbert J. Cuevas. Copyright © 1992 by GoodYearBooks.

SCOUTING OUTING

ACTIVITY 33

1. What do you need money for? (Teacher is expert for possible activities/costs.)

    a hamburger
    a soft drink
    a large order of fries
    the bus ride
    the bridge toll to the state park
    admission to the state park
    a locker at the park

2. What are the costs?

a hamburger	$1.59
a soft drink	.79
a large order of fries	.49
the bus ride	3.50
the bridge toll to the state park	.50
admission to the state park	2.75
a locker at the park	60
	$10.22

3. Can you afford to take this trip? Answers will vary. For the illustration given here, the students would need $0.22 more.

From *Primary Problem Solving in Math* by Jack A. Coffland and Gilbert J. Cuevas. Copyright © 1992 by GoodYearBooks.

HAPPY BIRTHDAY

▷ Stacy is planning her birthday party. At the party, her friends will play games, eat cake and ice cream, see her open presents, and watch a movie. Stacy's mother sent out party invitations that look like this:

COME TO STACY'S
9th BIRTHDAY
3:00 TO 5:00 P.M.

1. Will there be time to do all of the things Stacy wants to do?

   Activities Stacy would like to do

   _____   _____

   _____   _____

   _____   _____

   Time needed for each activity

   Activity: Time:

   _____   _____ min.

   _____   _____ min.

   _____   _____ min.

   _____   _____ min.

   _____   _____ min.

   _____   _____ min.

2. Can Stacy do all of this in 2 hours (120 minutes)?

   Yes, it will take _____   No, it takes _____

From *Primary Problem Solving in Math* by Jack A. Coffland and Gilbert J. Cuevas. Copyright © 1992 by GoodYearBooks.

HAPPY BIRTHDAY

Suggested activities: (Teacher is a time expert.)

Greet her friends
Play "Pin the Tail on the Donkey"
Play "Musical Chairs"
Have an egg toss
Eat cake and ice cream
Open presents
Clean up
Watch a video movie

Time needed for each activity:

Greet her friends	10 minutes
Play "Pin the Tail on the Donkey"	15 minutes
Play "Musical Chairs"	12 minutes
Have an egg toss	7 minutes
Eat cake and ice cream	25 minutes
Open presents	27 minutes
Clean up	8 minutes
Watch a video movie	45 minutes

Can Stacy do all of this in 2 hours? Answers will vary.

A VALENTINE GIFT

ACTIVITY 35

You have decided to make a pencil holder for a friend on Valentine's Day. Your teacher has given you an empty can to use as holder. Your job is to

1. decide how to decorate the holder

2. figure out how many decorating materials you will need

3. compute how much the decoration of the pencil holder will cost

Item   Cost

_____   _____

_____   _____

_____   _____

4. Now you would like to fill the pencil holder, but you need to know how many pencils you will need.

   First, estimate the answer _____

   Now use pencils to figure out the answer _____

5. Was there a difference between your answer and the estimate?

6. If each pencil costs 10¢, how much will it cost to fill the pencil holder?

From *Primary Problem Solving in Math* by Jack A. Coffland and Gilbert J. Cuevas. Copyright © 1992 by GoodYearBooks.

A VALENTINE GIFT

ACTIVITY 35

*H*ave children think of these and other possible decorative items. Ask children to estimate costs, but be ready to help.

Example List	Amount	Cost
paper to decorate the can	_____	_____
bows	_____	_____
ribbons	_____	_____
glitter	_____	_____
glue	_____	_____
tape	_____	_____
stickers	_____	_____

Have empty cans available in a variety of sizes along with plenty of pencils. After students have estimated the number of pencils needed, have them use pencils to check their estimates. They can then go on to compute the costs.

Extension:

Children can actually make the pencil holders planned in the problem.

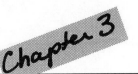

ALGORITHMIC PROBLEMS

Algorithmic Problems

*E*lementary school children must learn the series of steps necessary to perform the various computational operations in arithmetic. These steps or procedures are known as *computational algorithms*. The solution of "story" or word problems requires students to apply one of these algorithms. For this reason we refer to word problems as *algorithmic problems*. Characteristically, these problems:

■ require children to select and use a previously learned series of steps (an algorithm) in the solution,

■ are known as routine problems because they do not require students to be creative in developing a solution plan, and

■ are verbal representations of computational situations.

Examples:

Johnny takes $14 with him to the store. He buys a baseball for $8. How much money does he have left after his purchase?

Maria has 14 teddy bears in her collection. She gets 3 new teddy bears for Christmas. How many bears does she have in all?

Kawannah has 4 picture frames. Each frame holds 6 pictures. How many pictures can she display in her picture frames?

Instructional Considerations

Routine, algorithmic problems have been criticized as not requiring true problem-solving skills. However, algorithmic problems need to be a part of any program of problem-solving instruction. They show children applications for each of the operations, and they provide them with a useful set of skills that can be applied to non-routine problems. More specifically, routine problems provide:

■ practice in applying computational procedures to problem-solving situations,

■ opportunities to develop problem-solving skills in simple problem settings, and

■ experiences in problem-solving which can then be transferred to non-routine problems.

From *Primary Problem Solving in Math* by Jack A. Coffland and Gilbert J. Cuevas. Copyright © 1992 by GoodYearBooks.

Solving algorithmic problems should be part of the problem-solving instructional process, *but it is definitely not the final goal.*

Activity Objectives

The teaching suggestions and activities are designed to help students to:

- solve "story" problems requiring addition, subtraction, and multiplication, first using manipulatives and then working the problem with numerals only.

- state and apply a problem-solving strategy. Strategies included are:
  a. using a problem-solving strategy
  b. drawing a picture
  c. estimating a reasonable answer

- recognize difficulty factors that can be placed in a problem. Difficulty factors include:
  a. reverse order problems
  b. hidden number problems
  c. extra number problems

- follow strategies modeled by the teacher in order to complete problem-solving assignments.

Algorithmic Problems

ALL ABOUT TEDDY BEARS

ACTIVITY 36

Read the following problems to children. Ask them to arrange their teddy bear counters in the boxes shown on the worksheet on page 80 to illustrate and solve the problem. (Substitute other manipulatives if no teddy bear counters are available.)

Emphasize that all of these problems ask children to combine sets—to put the groups together. Illustrate that action by sweeping the sets of counters from the first two boxes into the answer box.

Try not to teach "key words." Instead, use—and encourage children to use—complete descriptive sentences in talking about the problems and their solutions. (You may wish to substitute your children's names for the names given in the problems.)

1. Maria has 3 teddy bear counters. She gets 1 more. How many does she have now? Show me what happens in this story.

2. Tommy has 2 teddy bear counters. Billy gives him 3 more. How many does Tommy have all together? Show me what happens in this story.

3. Sally has 1 teddy bear counter. Barbara gives her 2 more. How many does Sally have in all? Show me what happens in this story.

4. Kelly starts with 1 teddy bear counter. She gets 1 more from Andrew. How many does she have now? Show me what happens in this story.

5. Donna has 2 teddy bear counters. Then Mrs. Johnson gives her 1 more. How many does she have in total? Show me what happens in this story.

6. Richard has 3 teddy bear counters. Then Sam gives him 2 more. How many counters does Richard have in all? Show me what happens in this story.

From *Primary Problem Solving in Math* by Jack A. Coffland and Gilbert J. Cuevas. Copyright © 1992 by GoodYearBooks.

ADDING WITH CUBES

From *Primary Problem Solving in Math* by Jack A. Coffland and Gilbert J. Cuevas. Copyright © 1992 by GoodYearBooks.

R ead the following problems to children. Ask them to arrange their Unifix® cubes in the boxes shown on the worksheet on page 80 to illustrate and solve the problem. (Substitute other manipulatives if no Unifix® cubes are available.)

Emphasize that all of these problems ask children to combine sets—to put the groups together. Illustrate that action by sweeping the sets of counters from the first two boxes into the answer box. Then, have children push the smaller sets together to make the new, answer set.

Try not to teach "key words." Instead, use—and encourage children to use—complete descriptive sentences in talking about the problems and their solutions. (You may wish to substitute your children's names for the names given in the problems.)

Notice the variety of phrases used in these problems to indicate the operation of addition. Be certain that children connect all these phrases to the adding process.

1. Julio has 2 cubes. I give him 3 more. How many does he have in all? Show me what happens in this story.

2. Mike has 4 cubes. Suzy gives him 1 more. How many does he have now? Show me what happens in this story.

3. Tammy has 1 cube. She gets 2 more. What is the total number of cubes that Tammy has? Show me what happens in this story.

4. Andrea has 3 cubes. Melinda gives her 1 more. How many does Andrea have in all? Show me what happens in this story.

5. Marcy has 4 cubes. I give her 1 more. How many does Marcy have now? Show me what happens in this story.

6. Bobbi has 2 cubes. She gets 2 more. How many does Bobbi have in total? Show me what happens in this story.

DINOSAUR COUNTDOWN

ACTIVITY 38

R ead the following problems to children. Ask them to arrange their dinosaur counters in the boxes shown on the worksheet on page 80 to illustrate and solve the problem. (Substitute other manipulatives if no dinosaur counters are available.)

Emphasize that all of these problems ask children to combine sets—to put the groups together. Illustrate that action by sweeping the sets of counters from the first two boxes into the answer box. Then, have children push the smaller sets together to make the new, answer set.

Try not to teach "key words." Instead, use—and encourage children to use—complete descriptive sentences in talking about the problems and their solutions. (You may wish to substitute your children's names for the names given in the problems.)

Notice the variety of phrases used in these problems to indicate the operation of addition. Be certain that children connect all these phrases to the addition process.

Note: The numerals are slightly larger in this problem set; all sums are still kept to 8 or less.

1. Colette has 5 dinosaur counters. I give her 3 more. How many does she have in all? Show me what happens in this story.

2. Michelle has 4 dinosaur counters. Rachael gives her 2 more. How many does she have now? Show me what happens in this story.

3. Justin has 2 dinosaur counters. He gets 5 more. What is the total number of dinosaur counters that Justin has? Show me what happens in this story.

4. Sam has 3 dinosaur counters. Melinda gives him 3 more. How many does Sam have in all? Show me what happens in this story.

5. Marc has 4 dinosaur counters. I give him 4 more. How many does Marc have now? Show me what happens in this story.

Algorithmic Problems

6. Dianna has 6 dinosaur counters. She gets 1 more.
   What is the total number of counters that Dawn has? Show me what happens in this story.

Extension:

In the latter part of the first grade, emphasize the "reversibility" of addition:

1. Make two sets, and combine them to form the larger, answer set. For example, take a set of 2 and a set of 3; push them together to make the set of 5.

2. Then, tell children they can check their answer by using the take-away procedure. For example, using the worksheet with 5 counters in the answer box, take away 2 counters and put them back in the first box. Now count out 3 counters and put them in the second box. The answer 5 is correct since no counters are left in the answer box.

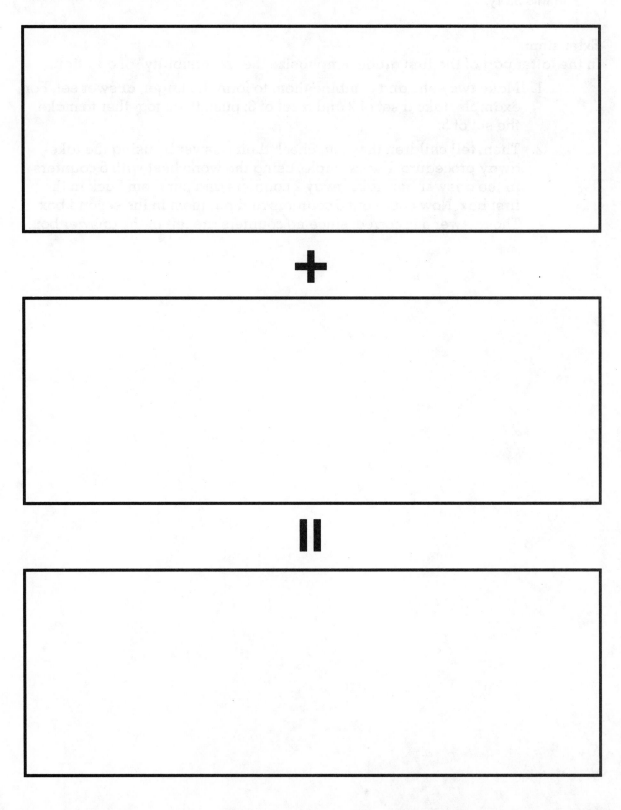

DINOSAUR DASH

$\mathcal{R}$ ead the following problems to children. Ask them to arrange their dinosaur counters in the boxes shown on the worksheet on page 84 to illustrate and solve the problem. (Substitute other manipulatives if no dinosaur counters are available.)

Emphasize that all of these problems ask children to take away part of a set—to subtract. Model the action of "taking away." Using the problem 4 - 1 = 3 as an example, have children place 4 counters in the first box on the reproducible page. Then ask them to take 1 counter away by moving it to the second box. Finally, have children move the counters that are left in the first box to the answer box. This box shows what is left after 1 is taken away. The answer is 3.

Try not to teach "key words." Instead, use—and encourage children to use—complete descriptive sentences in talking about the problems and their solutions. (You may wish to substitute your children's names for the names given in the problems.)

Problems:

1. Billy has 3 dinosaur counters. He gives 1 to Zach. How many does Billy have left?

2. Christie has 2 dinosaur counters. She takes 1 away. How many does she have now?

3. Sarah Beth has 3 dinosaur counters. She takes 2 of them away. How many dinosaur counters remain on her worksheet?

4. Robin has 2 dinosaur counters. He takes 2 off the paper. How many dinosaur counters are left?

5. Jim starts with 4 dinosaur counters. Then he takes 2 of them away. How many does he have now?

6. Kaitlin puts 3 dinosaur counters on her worksheet. Then she takes 2 of them off. How many are left on her page now?

Algorithmic Problems

BLOCKBUSTERS

R ead the following problems to children. Ask them to arrange their blocks in the boxes shown on the worksheet on page 84 to illustrate and solve the problem. (Substitute other manipulatives if no blocks are available.)

Emphasize that all of these problems ask children to take away part of a set—to subtract. Model the action of "taking away." Using the problem 4 - 1 = 3 as an example, have children place 4 blocks in the first box on the reproducible page. Then ask them to take 1 block away by moving it to the second box. Finally, have children move the blocks that are left in the first box to the answer box. This box shows what is left after 1 is taken away. The answer is 3.

Try not to teach "key words." Instead, use—and encourage children to use—complete descriptive sentences in talking about the problems and their solutions. (You may wish to substitute your children's names for the names given in the problems.)

Several different phrases are used in these problems to indicate the operation of subtraction. Be certain that children hear all of them in association with the subtraction process.

Problems:

1. Jeff has 5 blocks. He takes 2 of them away. How many blocks does he have now?

2. Billy has 4 blocks. I take 3 of them away. How many blocks does he have left?

3. Julio has 3 blocks. He gives 2 of them to John. How many blocks are left on Julio's page?

4. Maurice has 5 blocks. He gives 4 away. How many blocks remain on Maurice's worksheet?

5. Terry has 3 blocks on his page. He moves all 3 off the page. How many blocks are left on his page now?

6. Jim has 5 blocks. He shares 1 with Flo. How many does he have left?

SUBTRACTING WITH CUBES

ACTIVITY **41**

Read the following problems to children. Ask them to arrange their Unifix® cubes in the boxes shown on the worksheet on page 84 to illustrate and solve the problem. (Substitute other manipulatives if no cubes are available.)

- Emphasize that all of these problems ask children to take away part of a set—to subtract.

- Try not to teach "key words."

- Different phrases are used in these problems to indicate subtraction.

Problems:

1. Sammy puts 7 cubes in a row. Then he takes 3 of them away. How many does he have left?

2. Carl has 5 cubes on his worksheet. He takes 3 of them away. How many does he have now?

3. Randy has 8 cubes. He takes 5 of them away. How many does he have left?

4. Glenda makes a rod with 7 cubes. She takes 2 of them away. How many cubes does she have in her rod now?

5. Cindi puts 8 cubes on her paper. She uses 4 of them to make a rod. How many cubes are still on her paper?

6. David put 6 cubes on his paper. Then he gave 3 of them to Susan. How many does he have left?

Extension:
In the latter part of the first grade or in second grade, begin to stress the "reversibility" of subtraction. Using the problem 4 - 1 = 3 as an example, have children place 4 cubes in the first box on the reproducible page. Move 1 to the second box. Then move the cubes that are left in the first box to the answer box.

Emphasize that if we put the small sets back together, they will combine to make the first set. Push the sets of 1 and 3 back together, moving them to the first box. You will have 4 again. This checks your answer.

Activity Sheet for: Dinosaur Dash, Blockbusters, and Subtracting with Cubes

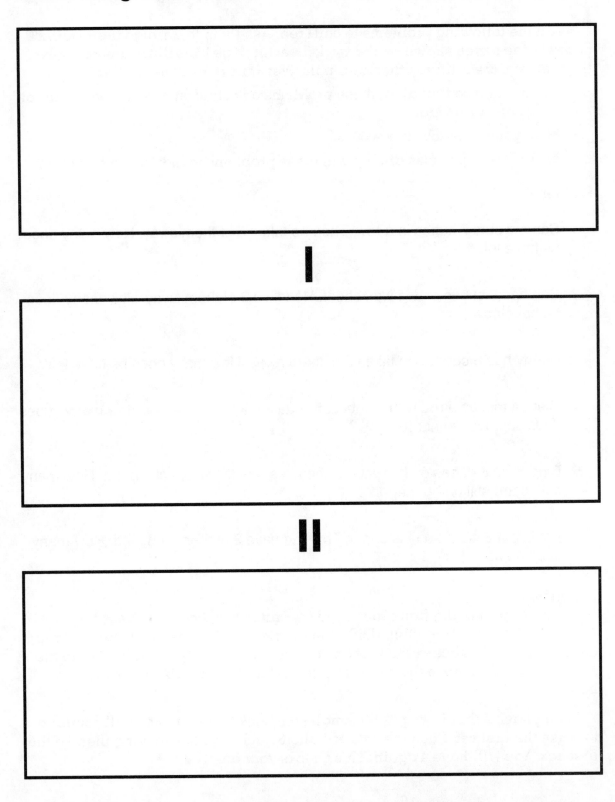

Algorithmic Problems

From *Primary Problem Solving in Math* by Jack A. Coffland and Gilbert J. Cuevas. Copyright © 1992 by GoodYearBooks.

MORE ABOUT TEDDY BEARS

ACTIVITY **42**

Read the following problems to children. Ask them to arrange their teddy bear counters in the boxes shown on the worksheet on page 88 to illustrate and solve the problem. (Substitute other manipulatives if no teddy bear counters are available.)

Emphasize that now the problems will require both addition and subtraction, so children must figure out which sign to put in the box. Copy the signs provided on this page for children's use.

1. Maria has 3 teddy bear counters. She gives 1 away. How many does she have left? Show me what happens in this story.

2. Tommy has 2 teddy bear counters. Greg gives him 3 more. How many does Tommy have now? Show me what happens in this story.

3. Ritika has 1 teddy bear counter. Barbara gives her 2 more. How many does Sally have now? Show me what happens in this story.

4. Lauren has 4 teddy bear counters. She takes 2 of them and gives them to David. How many does she have left? Show me what happens in this story.

5. Donna has 2 teddy bear counters. Then Mrs. Johnson gives her 1 more. How many does she have now? Show me what happens in this story.

6. Lori has 3 teddy bear counters. She gives 2 to Billy. How many does she have now? Show me what happens in this story.

Directions for Using the Signs: Have children cut out the two signs on their page and tape each sign to a small piece of tagboard. Have the children select the proper sign for each problem and place it in the sign box shown on the worksheet on page 88.

Algorithmic Problems

MORE BLOCKBUSTERS

ACTIVITY 43

R ead the following story problems to children. Using the worksheet on page 88, have them place the pattern blocks in the boxes as directed by the problem. Also, have them place the proper sign in the sign box.

1. Russell makes a shape with 3 green pattern blocks. Maurice makes his shape with 2 yellow blocks. How many blocks did the boys use in all? Show me what happens in this story.

2. Candy uses 4 red blocks to make a shape. Then she takes 1 of the blocks away. How many blocks are in her shape now? Show me what happens in this story.

3. Randy puts 4 yellow blocks on the board. Then he changes his mind and picks up 3 of the blocks. How many yellow blocks are left on his board? Show me what happens in this story.

4. Joanna experiments by making a shape out of 3 blues and 1 green. How many pattern blocks did she use in all? Show me what happens in this story.

5. Jaime uses 1 yellow and 3 blues to make a shape. How many pattern blocks did he use altogether? Show me what happens in this story.

TILE TACTICS

Read the following problems to children. Using the worksheet on page 88, have them place the tiles in the boxes as directed by the problem. Also, have them place the proper sign in the sign box.

The numbers in these problems are larger than on the preceding worksheet, but they do not exceed 8. Use other manipulatives if you do not have color tiles.

1. Melissa makes a shape with 6 red tiles. Then she adds 1 blue tile. How many tiles are in her shape now? Show me what happens in this story.

2. Cynthia used 5 red tiles and 3 green tiles to make a shape. How many tiles did she use in all? Show me what happens in this story.

3. Bobby put 8 yellow tiles on his board. That was too many. So he picked up 2. How many tiles were left on his board? Show me what happens in this story.

4. Cortez uses 7 green tiles to make a shape. Then he changes his mind and takes away 3 of the tiles. How many are left? Show me what happens in this story.

5. Kathy puts 2 red tile and 4 blue tiles on her board. How many tiles are on her board? Show me what happens in this story.

6. Gilberto uses 2 red tiles and 6 green tiles to make a shape. How many tiles did he use in all? Show me what happens in this story.

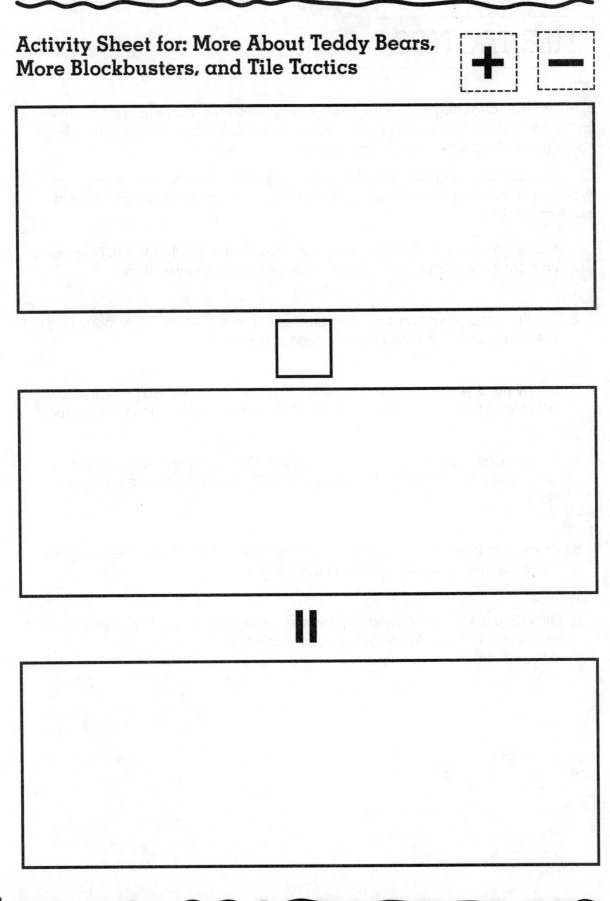

HOW MANY MORE?

ACTIVITY **45**

 Solve the following problems:

1. Gene has 9 pencils. Donna has 4 pencils. How many more pencils does Gene have?

2. Nancy has 8 special stamps. Bill has 6 of these special stamps. How many more stamps does Nancy have?

3. Bonnie has 8 old pennies. Her friend Bill gives her 4 more. How many old pennies does Bonnie have now?

4. Sally has 14 horses on her ranch. Bobby has 12 on his ranch. How many more horses does Sally have on her ranch?

5. Carole has 9 sheets of red paper. She also has 5 sheets of blue paper. How many sheets of colored paper does she have?

6. Sherry has 7 chores to do. Toni has 4 chores on her list. How many more chores does Sherry have to do?

HOW MANY MORE?

ACTIVITY 45

Children need practice in recognizing all subtraction situations. In the early grades, beginning exercises should stress the take-away model. But as children move up in age and ability, the other subtraction models should be introduced in algorithmic problem form. The first new model introduced should be the comparison model.

> Mindi has 7 teddy bears. David has 4. How many more teddy bears does Mindi have?

To solve this problem, make the two sets. Then demonstrate how Mindi has more bears. Match the bears in a one-to-one correspondence and indicate that three of Mindi's bears can not be matched. Therefore, Mindi has 3 more bears than David.

Young children often misunderstand the phrase "how many more," which can be found in a comparison problem. Use the phrase "how many extra" if that is the case. For many children the phrase "how many more" tells them to count the larger set, while "how many extra" tells them to find the difference between the sets.

Note that on the student page you will find both subtraction and addition questions (just to keep students thinking!).

THE MISSING ADDEND

▷ Solve the following problems:

1. Amy needs seven coupons to get a prize. She only has 3. How many more does she need?

2. Emilio has to work 10 hours every day. Today he has worked 7. How many hours does he have left to work?

3. Chiquita wants to buy a music tape. She has $7. The tape costs $15. How much more money does she need?

4. Mrs. Johnson's second-grade class is working on a project. The students want to buy a VCR for the class. They are collecting cereal box coupons. They have collected 60 coupons. They need 80. How many more coupons do they need to get the VCR?

5. Carl is working on a science project. He has a list of 18 books to read. He has read 11. How many more books does he have to read?

6. David has 7 mystery books. He gets 3 new ones for his birthday. How many books does he have now?

Algorithmic Problems

THE MISSING ADDEND

*T*here is one final subtraction story problem situation which requires special attention for children. It is called the "missing addend" problem.

Bobby has 4 paper airplanes finished. He wants to make 7 of them. How many does he have left to make?

This problem could be solved with an addition problem that looks like this:

$4 + \square = 7$

The child must find the number that is added to 4 to make 7; that number is the missing addend. In order to find the missing addend, he or she must write a subtraction number sentence that looks like this:

$7 - 4 = ?$

Writing a subtraction number sentence requires a reversal. Reversals cause many younger children difficulty; therefore, this activity is recommended for children in second grade and beyond. There is no reason to rush into missing addend problems; young children have sufficient subtraction algorithmic problem opportunities in subtraction with the take away and comparison situations.

Note: Remember that not all problems on this page are subtraction problems.

From *Primary Problem Solving in Math* by Jack A. Coffland and Gilbert J. Cuevas. Copyright © 1992 by GoodYearBooks.

USING QUESTIONS TO FIND ANSWERS

1. Marty has 3 tennis balls. She gets 3 more tennis balls. How many tennis balls does Marty have all together?

   Show work here: What did you do? (Circle one)

                                       Add +

                                       Subtract -

2. Karen has 9 storybook dolls. She gives 2 of them to her sister. How many dolls does she have left?

   Show work here: What did you do? (Circle one)

                                       Add +

                                       Subtract -

3. Bobby saved 6 pop bottles. Jamie saved 4 pop bottles. How many pop bottles do they have all together?

   Show work here: What did you do? (Circle one)

                                       Add +

                                       Subtract -

4. Don has 3 paper cups. Greg has 5 paper cups. How many paper cups do the boys have in all?

   Show work here: What did you do? (Circle one)

                                       Add +

                                       Subtract -

From *Primary Problem Solving in Math* by Jack A. Coffland and Gilbert J. Cuevas. Copyright © 1992 by GoodYearBooks.

USING QUESTIONS TO FIND ANSWERS

ACTIVITY 47

Students often have difficulty "getting started" on a problem. Whether this problem stems from an inability to solve the problem or an unwillingness to try, the effect is still the same: they seek help from the teacher. Giving these students a series of problem-solving steps to follow will get them started on their own.

The following questions are recommended to guide the students' thinking through the solution of a problem. After giving the students time to read the problem (or after you have read it to them), ask the following questions:

■ What are you looking for in this problem?

■ What information should you remember in this problem?

■ What do you have to do to answer the problem question?

■ Why did you choose this response?

■ After getting an answer, how can you check to see if you are correct?

These questions constitute what is referred to as a *heuristic procedure*. A heuristic procedure is a general problem-solving strategy which provides aid and direction to the problem solver. With these questions in mind, students can direct their thinking towards a process which leads to a solution. By giving this set of heuristics, *we are suggesting a strategy which can be used to solve both routine and non-routine problems.* In other words, skills practiced while solving algorithmic problems should lead toward skills used in solving non-routine problems. Use these questions as you work together with the children in solving each of the problems on page 93. Help children see how the answers lead them toward solutions.

From *Primary Problem Solving in Math* by Jack A. Coffland and Gilbert J. Cuevas. Copyright © 1992 by GoodYearBooks.

PUTTING THINGS IN ORDER

ACTIVITY 48

 Solve the following problems:

1. Melinda has 5 oranges. She shares 3 with her friends. How many does she have left?

2. Kathleen eats 3 pieces of popcorn. She had 8 pieces in her hand. How many pieces are left?

3. Terrence has 3 computer games. He gets 4 more for his birthday. How many games does he have altogether?

4. Ashley spends 2 pennies on gum. She had 7 pennies. How many pennies does she have now?

5. Tanya gives her friend 3 pieces of paper. She had 9 pieces in her notebook. How many pieces of paper are left in the notebook?

6. Joshua spent 3 dollars on a book. He went to town with 8 dollars. How many dollars does he have left?

Algorithmic Problems

PUTTING THINGS IN ORDER

ACTIVITY 48

*D*ifficulty factors can be written into algorithmic problems to make them harder for children to solve. Children should be taught to look for them; they can learn how to avoid being stymied or tricked by the difficulty factors.

The "difficulty factor" encountered first by most children is *reverse order* in subtraction problems. In reverse-order subtraction problems, the numerals are not presented in the order they are used. (This is only important in a subtraction problem for now. Order is not important in addition or multiplication because both are commutative operations.) Let's look at a right-order subtraction problem and a reverse-order problem.

Right Order

Sam has $8. He buys a

ball for $5. How much

money does he have left?

Number Sentence: 8 - 5 = ☐

Reverse Order

Sam buys a ball for $5. He has

$8. How much money will

he have left?

Number Sentence: 5 - 8 = ☐ ???

The right-order problem gives the 8, then the 5, and the question implies subtraction. It is easy for students to write 8 - 5 = ? In the reverse-order problem, the numeral 5 is given before the numeral 8. Students may write the number sentence as 5 - 8 = ?

Children can recognize and master the reverse-order problem by applying the following questions. These questions should help students STOP and THINK about the order in which the information must be placed in the number sentence in order to solve the problem.

■ What are you looking for in this problem?

■ What information should you remember in this problem?

■ What do you have to do to answer the problem question?

■ Why did you choose this response?

■ After getting an answer, how can you check to see if you are correct?

These questions should help students stop and think about the order in which the information must be placed in the number sentence in order to solve the problem.

From *Primary Problem Solving in Math* by Jack A. Coffland and Gilbert J. Cuevas. Copyright © 1992 by GoodYearBooks.

FINDING HIDDEN NUMBERS

ACTIVITY 49

 Solve the following problems:

1. Sarah Beth ate 3 pancakes for breakfast. Doug ate four. How many pancakes did they eat all together?

2. Kawannah took 8 pieces of candy on the field trip. She ate five before lunch. How many did she have left for the afternoon?

3. Debbie has five books in her desk. She takes 3 of them home to study. How many books are left in her desk?

4. There are seven balls in the closet. The class takes 5 of them out for recess. How many balls remain in the closet?

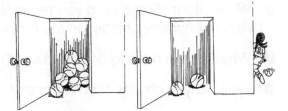

5. Aida invited four friends to her party. Her mother invited 3 children. How many guests were there at the party?

6. Doug had 8 toy cars. He gave three to his sister. How many does he have now?

Algorithmic Problems

FINDING HIDDEN NUMBERS

ACTIVITY 49

A very tricky way to make a problem more difficult is to hide some of the needed numbers. Instead of appearing as numerals as the children expect, the numbers appear as words. Hidden numbers represent another type of difficulty factor children can learn about and master. For example,

Easy Problem	**Hidden Number Problem**
Diane has 2 pet fish.	Diane has **two** pet fish.
Donna has 4 pet fish.	Donna has 4 pet fish.
How many fish do the girls have in all?	How many fish do the girls have in all?
Number Sentence: 2 + 4 = ☐	Number Sentence: ? + 4 = ☐

In the hidden number problem, the word *two*, not the numeral 2, tells how many fish Diane has.

Encourage children to become accustomed to looking for hidden numbers. These familiar questions can help. Notice, though, the addition of the new question on hidden numbers.

■ Read the problem. What are you looking for in this problem?

■ What information should you remember in this problem? Are any numbers hidden in the problem?

■ What do you have to do to answer the problem question?

■ Why did you choose this response?

■ After getting an answer, how can you check to see if you are correct?

From *Primary Problem Solving in Math* by Jack A. Coffland and Gilbert J. Cuevas. Copyright © 1992 by GoodYearBooks.

EXTRA! EXTRA!

▷ Solve the following problems:

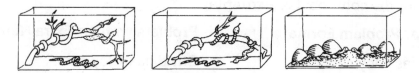

1. Barbara collects snakes. She has 3 of them. Her friend Larry has 4 snakes. But Donna collects turtles. She has 5 of them. How many snakes do Barbara and Larry have in all?

   Which numeral is not needed?   _____

   Which numerals should be used?   _____ _____

2. Bill is in Cabin 6 at camp. There are 8 boys and 2 adult counselors in his cabin. How many people are assigned to Bill's cabin?

   Which numeral is not needed?   _____

   Which numerals should be used?   _____ _____

3. Marianne spent 2 weeks at camp. She went out on the lake 4 times in a rowboat. She also went down the river in a canoe 5 times. How many boat trips did Marianne take all together?

   Which numeral is not needed?   _____

   Which numerals should be used?   _____ _____

4. Dan went to the football game on October 20. He and his Dad ate 5 hot dogs. If Dan ate 3 of the hot dogs, how many did his father eat?

   Which numeral is not needed?   _____

   Which numerals should be used?   _____ _____

EXTRA! EXTRA!

Problems are more difficult for students if they include numbers that are not needed for for the solution. For example:

Familiar Problem Format

David has 4 toy cars.

Billy has 3 toy cars.

How many cars do David and Billy have all together?

Problem with an Extra Number

David has 4 toy cars.

Billy has 3 toy cars.

Elizabeth has 2 toy cars.

How many toy cars do David and Billy have all together?

The question does not ask how many cars Elizabeth has; the fact that Elizabeth has 2 toy cars is extra information.

It is important for students to pay close attention to the information given in a problem. The problem-solving questions children have been learning to use will help them accomplish this. Have children use these questions as they work through the problems on page 99. Draw their attention to the new question on extra information.

■ Read the problem. What are you looking for in this problem?

■ What information should you remember in this problem?
   What information is not needed to solve this problem?

■ What do you have to do to answer the problem question?

■ Why did you choose this response?

■ After getting an answer, how can you check to see if you are correct?

These questions should help students STOP and THINK as they evaluate the relevance of the information in the story problem question.

PROBLEM-SOLVING PICTURES

ACTIVITY **51**

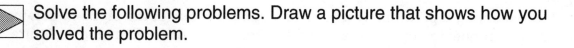

Solve the following problems. Draw a picture that shows how you solved the problem.

1. Dawn has 5 pieces of paper. She writes on 3 of them. How many does she have left?

2. Matt has 4 gumdrops. He gets 5 more out of the bag. How many gumdrops does he have in all?

3. Elaine has 7 pencils for school. She loses 4 of them. How many pencils does she have left for school?

4. Patrick has 3 apples. He buys 5 more at the grocery store. How many apples does he have all together?

From *Primary Problem Solving in Math* by Jack A. Coffland and Gilbert J. Cuevas. Copyright © 1992 by GoodYearBooks.

PROBLEM-SOLVING PICTURES | ACTIVITY 51

Representing a problem by means of a picture is one of the problem-solving strategies suggested by experts in mathematics education. Drawing a picture or a diagram which represents a word problem will help students visualize the information given and aid in the solution process. Consider the following problem: (Either use actual toys to act out the story, or draw it on the board with the children.)

Joey has 8 toy cars. He gives 3 of them away. How many will he have left?

Draw or use eight toy cars.

Then cross out or remove three of them.

Children can see that there are five cars left.

Note: With younger children you may wish to use toys or other manipulatives to represent the problems.

LEARNING ABOUT MULTIPLICATION

PROBLEM ANSWER

▷ Solve the following problems:

1. Marty has 3 cans of tennis balls. Each can holds 3 tennis balls. How many tennis balls does Marty have all together?

   _____ Is this an addition problem?   Show your work here:

   _____ Is this a subtraction problem?

   _____ Is this a multiplication problem?

2. Karen has 9 storybook dolls. She gives 2 of them to her sister. How many dolls does she have left?

   _____ Is this an addition problem?   Show your work here:

   _____ Is this a subtraction problem?

   _____ Is this a multiplication problem?

3. Bobby saved 6 pop bottles. Jessica saved 4 pop bottles. How many pop bottles do they have all together?

   _____ Is this an addition problem?   Show your work here:

   _____ Is this a subtraction problem?

   _____ Is this a multiplication problem?

4. Don has 3 stacks of paper cups. Each stack has 5 cups in it. How many paper cups does Don have all together?

   _____ Is this an addition problem?   Show your work here:

   _____ Is this a subtraction problem?

   _____ Is this a multiplication problem?

LEARNING ABOUT MULTIPLICATION

Multiplication can be called "repeated addition." You could add to get the answer to a multiplication problem, but you might have to add the same number many times. An example looks like this:

> Frances buys 4 boxes of golf balls. Each box holds 3 golf balls. How many golf balls did she get all together?

Use actual boxes and balls to demonstrate this situation. Fill 4 boxes with 3 balls each. Tell children that one way to find the total number of golf balls is by adding:

> 3 golf balls + 3 golf balls + 3 golf balls + 3 golf balls = ? golf balls.

But go on to say that you could just as easily multiply, like this:

> 4 boxes X 3 golf balls in each box = 12 golf balls all together

Remind children that when they solve the problems on page 103, they should look especially carefully at the multiplication problems. They should remember to solve them by multiplying, not adding. Remind them that they may find addition and subtraction problems also.

LEARNING MORE ABOUT MULTIPLICATION

▷ Solve the following problems:

1. Janie has 5 big square blocks. She wants to pair them with 2 small triangle blocks. How many combinations can she make?

   _____ Is this an addition problem?   Show your work here:

   _____ Is this a subtraction problem?

   _____ Is this a multiplication problem?

2. A space monster has 4 feet. It wants to have 3 shoes for each foot. How many shoes does she need for that?

   _____ Is this an addition problem?   Show your work here:

   _____ Is this a subtraction problem?

   _____ Is this a multiplication problem?

3. Yamika goes to town with $8. She spends $3 on a new purse. How much money does she have left?

   _____ Is this an addition problem?   Show your work here:

   _____ Is this a subtraction problem?

   _____ Is this a multiplication problem?

4. Tad has 3 swimming suits. He also has 3 shirts that he wears after swimming. How many different outfits can he make?

   _____ Is this an addition problem?   Show your work here:

   _____ Is this a subtraction problem?

   _____ Is this a multiplication problem?

LEARNING MORE ABOUT MULTIPLICATION

ACTIVITY 53

Another way children need to look at multiplication is to make a Cartesian cross-product between two sets in which every element of one set is paired with every element of another set. For example:

> Dennis has three shirts and two pairs of jeans that go together. How many outfits can he make from these clothes?

Here we have to pair every shirt with every pair of pants. To do this we will use a chart:

	White Shirt	Blue Shirt	Red Shirt
Blue Pants	B/W	B/B	B/R
White Pants	W/W	W/B	W/R

You can see that when the set of three shirts is paired with a set of two pants, we have six different outfits to wear. In other words $3 \times 2 = 6$.

An important question to ask is "Are the outfits all different?" Consider the B/W outfit and the W/B outfit. One contains a blue pair of pants and a white shirt, while the other contains a white pair of pants and a blue shirt. They are different.

Problems of this type are found in the practice page, but not all problems are multiplication problems. Children must review each problem carefully, even to deciding which process is needed.

LET'S GO FLY A KITE

ACTIVITY **54**

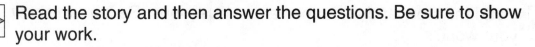 Read the story and then answer the questions. Be sure to show your work.

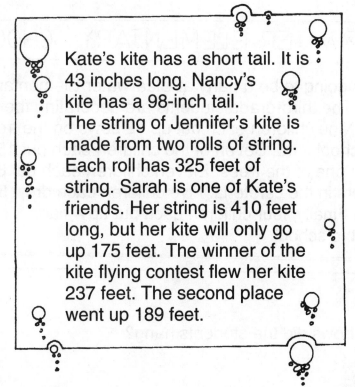

Kate's kite has a short tail. It is 43 inches long. Nancy's kite has a 98-inch tail. The string of Jennifer's kite is made from two rolls of string. Each roll has 325 feet of string. Sarah is one of Kate's friends. Her string is 410 feet long, but her kite will only go up 175 feet. The winner of the kite flying contest flew her kite 237 feet. The second place went up 189 feet.

1. How much longer is Nancy's kite tail than Kate's?

2. How much string does Jennifer have?

3. When Sarah's kite would not go any higher, how much string did she have left in the roll?

4. How much higher did the winner's kite fly than Sarah's kite?

From *Primary Problem Solving in Math* by Jack A. Coffland and Gilbert J. Cuevas. Copyright © 1992 by GoodYearBooks.

PARTY TIME

 Read the story and then answer the questions. Be sure to show your work.

CLEARWATER ELEMENTARY SCHOOL

There is going to be a party at Clearwater Elementary School. The third-grade students are decorating the school. Nine children each put up 12 bows on the trees in the school yard. Seven of the children each put 15 lights on one of the trees. Eleven children each put 8 streamers in the cafeteria. Five children each drew 5 posters. Finally, four children each put up 4 flags around the school.

1. How many bows did the students hang?

2. How many lights did the students put up on the tree?

3. How many streamers did the students hang in the cafeteria?

4. How many flags were put around the school?

From *Primary Problem Solving in Math* by Jack A. Coffland and Gilbert J. Cuevas. Copyright © 1992 by GoodYearBooks.

LET'S GO FLY A KITE AND PARTY TIME

*T*hese two activities represent algorithmic problems contained in lengthy stories. They are designed to give students an opportunity to process and use quantitative information. In addition, the problems contain some of the difficulty factors discussed in this chapter. These problems (or similar ones) could be used to assess how well students read and solve algorithmic problems.

Remind students to review the following problem-solving questions as they respond to the questions posed in the activities:

■ Read the problem. What are you looking for in this problem?

■ What information should you remember in this problem?
Are any numbers hidden in the problem?

■ What do you have to do to answer the problem question?

■ Why did you choose this response?

■ After getting an answer, how can you check to see if you are correct?

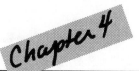
Chapter 4

TRANSITIONAL ACTIVITIES

Transitional Activities

$\mathcal{S}$tudent proficiency in problem solving is an important goal of mathematics instruction. A math program for young children should stress understanding mathematical ideas over the memorization of number facts and computational operations.

The transitional activities in this chapter are designed to help children understand numbers and to bridge the gap between computation and problem solving. These activities:

■ provide experiences to help students understand numbers, numerals, and the number system,

■ provide models for understanding the operations of addition, subtraction, multiplication, and division,

■ promote an understanding of how numerals and operations relate to actual life experiences, and

■ provide background skills needed to solve word problems in later grades.

These types of experiences should make math real for students. Problems of this sort must be structured in contexts that can later be related to all problem-solving activities. Following are examples of transitional activities.

1. Make a stack of 3 blocks and tell a story about 3.

2. Use your blocks to illustrate subtraction as "taking away" part of a set.

3. Solve the following problems (using manipulatives):

```
   2  blocks              12  tiles in a box
 +3  blocks             x 3  boxes
 _____           _____
   How many blocks         How many tiles
   all together?           all together?
```

4. Find the correct sign:

```
   2  blocks
 □ 3  blocks
 _____
   How many blocks in all?
```

From *Primary Problem Solving in Math* by Jack A. Coffland and Gilbert J. Cuevas. Copyright © 1992 by GoodYearBooks.

Instructional Considerations

Manipulative or concrete materials should be used throughout the teaching of problem-solving skills, but it is vital that these materials be used with young students working with transitional activities. Manipulative materials will:

■ help students conceptualize models of operations,

■ provide a context for relating numbers and operations to "real life,"

■ help develop language skills needed for problem solving, and

■ help children see relationships between number concepts, operations, and real-life number problems.

Generally, activities with manipulatives should always precede written activities. Some of the pages in this chapter are designed to be used with manipulative materials, while others should be implemented after concepts or ideas have been introduced with concrete objects.

Activity Objectives

Numeracy Section: The four activities in this section are designed to help children:

■ recognize number as an aspect of a set and to relate numerals to those real world objects, and

■ use manipulatives to relate numerals to sets.

Models for Operations: Suggestions and activities in this section lead children to constructing various models for each of the four basic operations with whole numbers.

Addition — Put two sets together (union of non-intersecting sets)

Subtraction — Removing a subset, comparing two sets, or finding the missing addend (three types of subtraction story problems)

Multiplication — Joining together of equivalent sets (Cartesian cross-product and repeated addition)

Division — Division as the inverse of multiplication, and division in two types of story problems (measurement and partition)

Introducing Computation and Problem-Solving Together: The teaching suggestions and activities in this section help children:

■ use the models for operations to represent number sentences for addition, subtraction, and multiplication,

■ select the appropriate operation given two quantities of objects and a question about the number of objects, and

■ label the result of an operation using the objects given in the operation.

DEVELOPING NUMBER SENSE

In developing children's abilities to understand what numerals mean, keep in mind that children:

- ■ always relate the numerals they use to real-life objects and experiences,

- ■ begin to learn numerals using numbers 1 – 5, followed by 6 – 10. They should learn about larger numbers in groups also.

- ■ need to learn that numerals stand for the quantity or amount of objects, and

- ■ explore number concepts through the manipulation of concrete objects.

Following are suggestions you may wish to use.

1. Classroom Situations: Use concrete classroom number situations to introduce children to the world of numerals.

   a. Buy two hula hoops. Place three children in one hoop, and two in another. Discuss the number of children in each hula hoop. Repeat often with different numbers.

   b. Count children whenever possible. Examples:
      - ■ There are 5 children at this table.
      - ■ There are 6 children in this group.
      - ■ I want 2 children to line up by the door.

   c. Emphasize the use of numbers and numerals when taking role, lunch counts, or other such classroom activities. Examples:
      - ■ There are 14 boys. Two boys are absent.
      - ■ Six girls want hot lunch. Ten girls brought bag lunches.
      - ■ There are 4 girls absent. There are 2 boys absent.

   d. Use numbers and numerals with common classroom objects. For example:
      - ■ Jon, I want you to get 4 books.
      - ■ Count out 3 pencils.
      - ■ How many color crayons are in this box?
      - ■ Get 2 pieces of paper.

Be sure to use numbers and/or numerals throughout the day. Use every possible opportunity to include number concepts in lessons across the curriculum.

2. Manipulative Materials: Using any common
   container, give children a "bank" filled with manipulatives. Objects
   may include buttons, chips, blocks, small toys, and/or color tiles. The
   following are examples of activities which illustrate the use of
   manipulatives with number concepts.

a. Write **2** on the board.

   ■ Make or draw sets of several different numbers. Have
   them find the set with 2 elements.

   ■ Draw pictures of sets of 2 on the board. Have children
   match your picture with their manipulatives.

   ■ Draw pictures of sets on the board. Have children make
   a set with "one more" or "one less."

   ■ Have children count out 2 objects and put them into a
   set.

   ■ Have children count out "the next number after 2."

   ■ Have children count out "one more" or "one less" than 2.
   Repeat with other numerals of 5 or less.

b. Write **8** on the board.

   Have children complete activities similar to those shown
   above using numerals 6 – 10.

   Please note that many children have an intuitive
   knowledge of numerals 1 – 5. Having them move on to
   larger sets requires them to extend that knowledge.

c. Repeat with numerals from **11** through **20**.

(Note: Do not be in a hurry to move on to larger numerals.)

Generally, activity pages should be done after numbers and their corresponding numerals have been introduced with manipulatives. Activities 56–59 can be used to introduce the idea that classifying objects can be accomplished by using numbers. We can count out sets with red objects, or sets of triangles, or we can find sets that have 2 objects in them—all are acceptable ways of classifying objects. For children having difficulty counting objects, these pages might be done before the manipulative activities.

LOOK ALIKES

ACTIVITY **56**

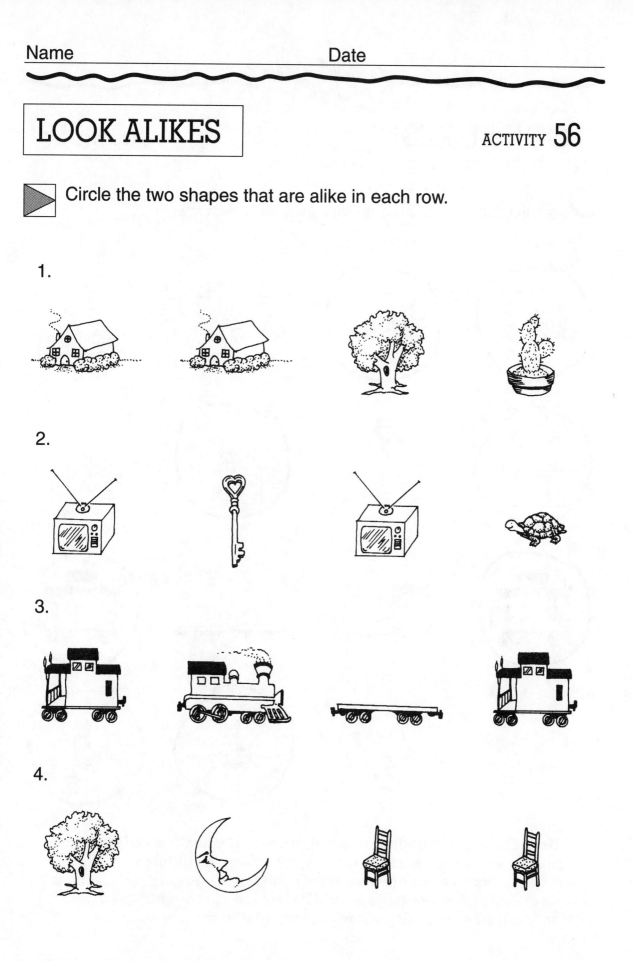

Circle the two shapes that are alike in each row.

1.

2.

3.

4.

LOOK ALIKES

Directions: Circle the two shapes that are alike in each row.

Note: Exercises in finding things that are the "same" or "different" ask children to classify items according to similarities and differences. When we speak of number sets, we are also asking children to classify, but by amount. Simple classification exercises should be included in the math program. The best way to do these activities is with manipulative materials.

LOOK OUT!

▷ Look at each line of objects. Circle the picture or set of pictures that is different. Tell the teacher why it is different.

1.

2.

3.

4.

LOOK OUT!

ACTIVITY **57**

Look at each line of objects. Circle the picture of set of pictures that is different. Tell the teacher why it is different.

1. **Answer:** Arrow is different.

2. **Answer:** Different and larger can.

3. **Answer:** A boy, not a girl.

4. **Answer:** Last pencil is not straight up and down.

Make certain children can explain why the selected item or group of items is different. They should practice describing the differences in words since communicating mathematical ideas is important.

From *Primary Problem Solving in Math* by Jack A. Coffland and Gilbert J. Cuevas. Copyright © 1992 by GoodYearBooks.

MAKING A MATCH

Color the sets in each row that contain the same number.

1.

2.

3.

4.

MAKING A MATCH

ACTIVITY 58

Children should learn to classify items as being the same by looking at the number of objects in a set. By doing this, they are classifying by number, not by size or shape or other attributes.

This activity asks children to classify sets as being the same based upon the number of items in the sets. If a child is having trouble with this type of classification, ask him or her to count the number of items in each set. Activities such as this should be performed with manipulatives before written exercises are given.

Extension:

1. Using yarn and objects on a felt board, make sets which have the same properties as those shown on this page (two sets with the same amount, two with differing amounts). Ask children to find the sets which are the same.

2. Place manipulatives (blocks, colored tiles, etc.) on sheets of construction paper. Use sets with the same properties as those shown on this page (two sets with the same amount, two with differing amounts). Ask children to find the sets that are the same.

3. Put a numeral on the board (for example, 3). Ask children to find sets representing that numeral from objects in the classroom. This activity could also be done on the playground. Give children cards with large numerals written on them. Ask the children to name things (sets) that have that amount (e.g., 3 slides, 3 swings, 3 friends).

From *Primary Problem Solving in Math* by Jack A. Coffland and Gilbert J. Cuevas. Copyright © 1992 by GoodYearBooks.

WHICH SET IS DIFFERENT?

ACTIVITY 59

▷ Color the set in each row that contains a different number than the other sets in the row.

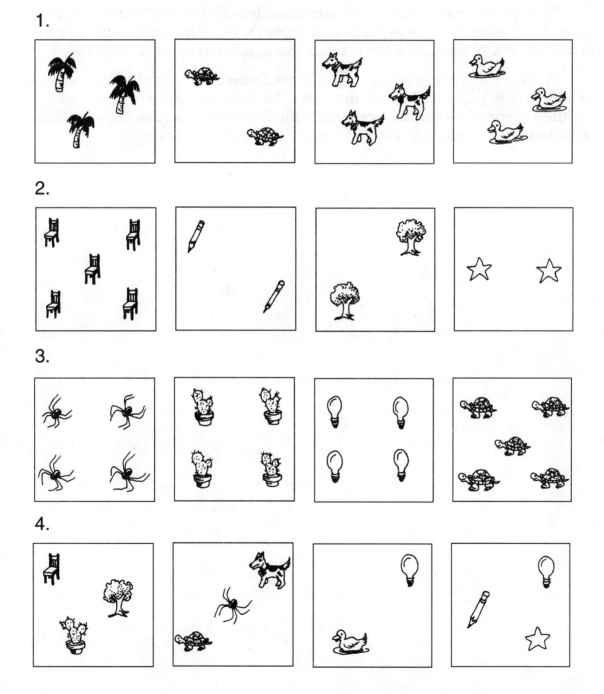

1.

2.

3.

4.

WHICH SET IS DIFFERENT?

Children should learn to classify items as being different by looking at the number of objects in a set. The classification system stressed here uses number, not size, shape, or other set attributes.

This activity page asks children to classify sets as being different based upon the number of items in the sets. If a child is having trouble with this type of classification, ask him or her to count the number of items in each set.

Similar kinds of exercises should be performed with manipulatives before activities with paper and pencil are given. So, before doing this page, ask children to complete similar exercises with manipulatives. See the extension activities listed under Activity 58 for ideas to expand these skills.

USING MODELS FOR OPERATIONS WITH WHOLE NUMBERS

Children need to develop the concepts for each of the operations with whole numbers. Applications of these concepts help children interpret and select the solution to word problems.

Operations can be represented concretely, symbolically, and verbally. For example:

(concrete),

- $4 + 2 = 6$ (symbolic), and
- four plus two equals six (verbal)

All express the same operation.

There are standard models used to represent each of the operations. In this section, the following models will be presented with teaching suggestions and activities:

- Addition as the union of non-intersecting sets
- Subtraction as "take-away"
- Subtraction as comparison
- Subtraction as the missing addend
- Multiplication as repeated additions
- Multiplication as a Cartesian Product
- Division as repeated subtractions
- Division as partition

Throughout the activities, there is an emphasis on giving children opportunities to make connections between the operation and the corresponding concrete, symbolic, and verbal representations. In addition, Activities 74–83 are presented as worksheets to give students additional exercises on making the transition from the idea of each operation to the various representations for the operation.

ADDITION NUMBER SENTENCES

Addition can be represented as the union of non-intersecting sets; it is the joining of elements of sets with no common elements. Children need many concrete examples showing that addition puts the elements of sets together into one new, larger set. Children also need to understand the abstract, symbolic way to represent this process.

Look at this example which uses manipulative materials (toys, chips, blocks). Here a concrete representation is paired with the abstract.

Concrete   Abstract

$2 + 3$

$= 5$

Follow this teaching strategy in helping children link the abstract with the concrete:

1. Use an example that combines the elements of two sets of concrete objects into a new, larger set (like the one above). At the same time, show the number sentence for the operation. Repeat with different objects and number sentences.

2. Convert the concrete representation into a simple story problem:

   John has 2 turtles and Mary has 3 turtles. They put all of the turtles into a dish. There are 5 turtles in the dish.

   Act out the situation with manipulatives. Repeat often with new story situations for any given number sentence.

3. Have children make up their own stories for the situation pictured above and for other concrete representations. Be sure to use examples *which show the connection between objects, number sentences, and words.* This activity should be done regularly before teaching abstract number combinations.

SUBTRACTION AS TAKE-AWAY | ACTIVITY 61

Subtraction as "take-away" involves the removal of a subset from a set of objects. This is usually the easiest model of subtraction for children to understand. Here is an example for presenting this particular model of subtraction to children.

Concrete (manipulatives)

Abstract

5 - 1

= 4

Use the following teaching strategy in helping children understand this subtraction model:

1. Show the concrete representation paired with the corresponding symbolic number sentence. Emphasize the action of "taking away" one of the objects. Repeat for different number sentences.

2. Turn each representation into a story problem. For the above illustration, the problem could be as follows:

   Johnny has 5 turtles. He gives 1 to Jenny. He has 4 turtles left.

3. Have children tell other stories which correspond with this number sentence.

4. Make up additional examples which show the connection between objects, number sentences, and words. Do exercises of this type regularly with young children.

SUBTRACTION AS COMPARISON

*T*his second model of subtraction stresses the comparison of the amounts in two sets. The child is asked to find how many more elements are in the larger set.

Concrete (manipulatives)

Billie Jean

Debbie

Abstract

$4 - 3 = 1$

Consider the teaching strategy:

1. As with the other models, the concrete representation is paired with the corresponding symbols. Here the required action is that of pairing the dogs in a one-to-one correspondence in order to see how many dogs are left over. Obviously, in the example given above, the child can pair three sets of dogs and then has 1 left over in Billie Jean's row.

2. Turn the representation into a story problem.

   Billie Jean has 4 dogs. Debbie has 3 dogs. How many more dogs does Billie Jean have?

   Note: Children often have problems with the question "How many more?" If you find that a child always names the number in the larger set as the answer to this question, you might want to try the following question for the example given above: "How many extra dogs does Billie Jean have?" The substitution of "how many extra" for "how many more" seems to help younger children. However, the teacher should interchange the phrases in order to teach children they mean the same thing.

3. Repeat with different sets and number sentences.

Transitional Activities

SUBTRACTION AS MISSING ADDEND

In subtraction as finding a missing addend, two sets are compared in order to determine how many more elements are needed to make them equal in size.

Concrete (manipulatives)   Abstract

David has:

$$6 - 4 = 2$$

David wants:

How many more cars does he need to make the train the size he wants?

1. As you pair the concrete representation with the number sentence, include a story about the illustration such as:

   David has a train with 4 cars. He wants to make a train with 6 cars. How many more cars does he need?

2. Make up additional missing addend examples which show the same connection between objects, number sentences, and words.

Note: This model of subtraction may be difficult for younger children. Keep the following in mind:

- Don't give this model to students too soon. For kindergarten and first-grade children, time is better spent mastering the "take away" and "comparison" models.

- Children may need more practice with this subtraction model than with the other two presented here.

MULTIPLICATION AS REPEATED SUBTRACTION

ACTIVITY **64**

Multiplication can be represented as repeated addition. The elements of various sets of equal size are added together to find the total number of elements in the new, larger set.

Three rows of four ducks.

Concrete   Abstract   Abstract

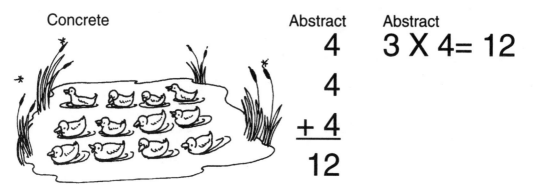

$$
\begin{array}{r}
4 \\
4 \\
+\,4 \\
\hline
12
\end{array}
$$

$3 \times 4 = 12$

Follow these steps in helping children understand that multiplication is the same as repeated addition.

1. As with addition and subtraction, pair a concrete representation with the abstract number sentence.

2. Use a story problem to illustrate each representation. A story problem for the above example could be:

   There are three rows of ducks swimming in the lake. Each row has 4 ducks in it. How many ducks are there all together?

3. Create additional examples and ask students to provide the story. Be sure to stress how the concrete illustration, the number sentence, and the story all describe the same operation.

4. You might also want to point out to your students that although the answers to problems like this one can be obtained through addition, they can be found more quickly through multiplication.

From *Primary Problem Solving in Math* by Jack A. Coffland and Gilbert J. Cuevas. Copyright © 1992 by GoodYearBooks.

MULTIPLICATION AS A CARTESIAN PRODUCT

Multiplication can also be represented as a Cartesian cross-product of two sets. A Cartesian cross-product requires the pairing of each element of one set with every element of the other set. The following example illustrates this model:

> How many different dessert combinations can you make if you have 2 kinds of cake and 3 kinds of ice cream?
>
> Two cakes   = chocolate and white
>
> Three ice creams   = chocolate, vanilla, and strawberry

Follow these steps in presenting problems liked this one:

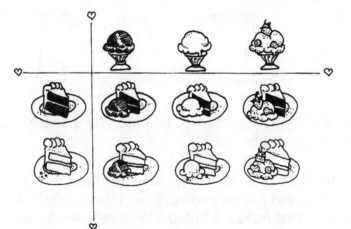

1. Prepare a chart like the one above. Use either the chalkboard or flannelboard cutouts.

2. Create a corresponding story problem:

   You have two kinds of cake and three kinds of ice cream. How many different combinations of dessert can you make using these cakes and ice creams?

3. Have the children name each of the different possibilities. (To do this, however, the sets need to be kept small.)

4. Make up similar problems (for example, shirts with pants or skirts, sandwich ingredients, etc.).

DIVISION AS MEASUREMENT DIVISION (REPEATED SUBTRACTION)

ACTIVITY 66

In this model, the total number of elements in a set is known. The size of the subsets in which the set is to be divided is also known. The object is to find the *number of subsets*. For example:

Mary wished to fill several vases with flowers. She has six flowers [*the total number in the set*]. She wants to put two flowers in each vase [*the size of the subsets*]. How many vases will she need [*the number of subsets*]?

Representation:

1. Using this conceptualization, the procedure for obtaining a solution to a division problem is through repeated subtraction.

   I put two flowers in the first vase. Now, how many do I have left? Let's see: 6-2=4. Then I put 2 flowers in the second vase, and that's 4-2=2. And two flowers in the third vase, that makes it 2-2=0. No more flowers. So I used three vases. The answer is 3.

2. Repeat with other story problems. Have students go through the process with manipulatives.

Note: The key to helping students recognize division as repeated subtraction is to use the same kind of units in the problem. You must be able to subtract flowers from flowers, toys from toys, etc.

DIVISION AS PARTITION

(DEALING OUT THE ELEMENTS)

ACTIVITY **67**

I n this model, the total number of elements in a set is given; so is the number of subsets into which the elements will be distributed. The object is to find the *size of the subsets*. The following example illustrates this model:

Tom wanted to share his toy cars with 3 friends [*number of subsets*]. Tom had 9 toy cars [*the total number of objects in the set*]. If Tom gave the same amount of cars to each of his friends, how many toy cars did each friend get [*the size of the subsets*]?

Representation:

How many cars for each friend?

1. This problem can be solved by distributing or "dealing out" the total number of elements among the number of subsets.

   I will start by "dealing out" the cars to the 3 friends until I run out of cars. I will count how many cars each friend has. Then I'll have my answer.

2. Repeat with other story problems. Have students go through the process with manipulatives.

Note: Because this model is more difficult, present it after working with the model of division as repeated subtraction.

COMBINING SETS

M*aterials:* Addition Worksheet (page 135), blocks, beans, chips, or other objects to be used in counting.

Directions:

- ■ Place 6 or 7 counters in the Bank space.
- ■ Draw a model of the student worksheet on the blackboard.
- ■ Write a numeral (3) on the board, then draw shapes in the first box to match the numeral.
- ■ Have children place 3 manipulatives inside the first box on their worksheets.
- ■ Expand the number sentence on the board to say 3 + 1; then draw 1 object in the second box.
- ■ Have children place 1 object inside the second box.
- ■ Complete the number sentence 3 + 1 = ??
- ■ As students move their manipulatives into the answer box, stress the fact that: "When we add, we have to combine sets."

Note: Initial activities should always have sums of 5 or less. As children become proficient at working with the concept of combining sets, gradually increase the size of the sums.

From *Primary Problem Solving in Math* by Jack A. Coffland and Gilbert J. Cuevas. Copyright © 1992 by GoodYearBooks.

Addition Sheet: Combining Sets

Bank

Box 1	Box 2

Answer Box

From *Primary Problem Solving in Math* by Jack A. Coffland and Gilbert J. Cuevas. Copyright © 1992 by GoodYearBooks.

BUILDING NUMBER SENTENCES ABOUT ADDITION

M aterials: Addition Worksheet (page 137), blocks, beans, chips, or other objects to be used in counting. It is a good idea to laminate the numerals for longer usage.

Directions:

- ■ Distribute copies of the student worksheet and have students cut out the numerals.

- ■ Draw the student page on the board. Draw 1 object in the first box. Have students place 1 object in the first box on their worksheets.

- ■ Say, "Now let's use numerals to show what we are doing with our objects." Write a 1 in the first number sentence box on the chalkboard. Have students select the 1 from their cut-out numerals and place it in the corresponding box on their worksheets.

- ■ Draw 4 objects in the second box on the board. Have students place 4 objects in the box on their activity page. Count the objects, and then write 4 in the number sentence box on the board. Have the children use the 4 from their cut-out numerals and place it in their number sentence box.

- ■ Finally, discuss the number sentence so far: $1 + 4 = ?$. Stress the fact that addition asks for a combination of sets—they will need to make a new, larger set which combines both of the previous sets. Combine 1 and 4 to make a new set of 5. Place 5 objects in the answer box; write the 5 in the number sentence answer box. Have the children do the same with real objects and the cut-out numeral.

- ■ Repeat, progressively using larger numbers, but continuing with the manipulatives and the cut-out numerals. Sums should be kept small in the beginning. Increase the size of the sums gradually.

Addition Sheet: Building Number Sentences About Addition

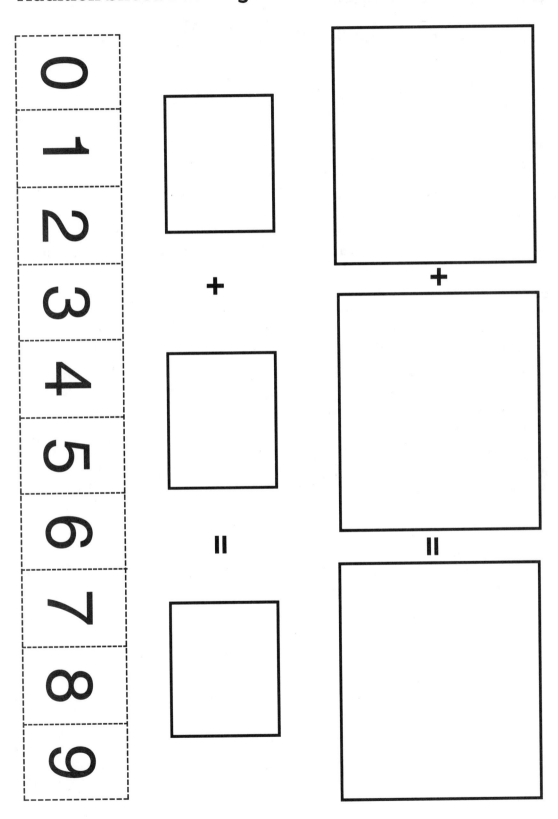

WRITING NUMBER SENTENCES ABOUT ADDITION

M*aterials:* Addition Worksheet (page 139), blocks, beans, chips, or other objects to be used in counting.

Directions:

- ■ Distribute copies of the student worksheet.

- ■ Draw the worksheet on the chalkboard. Draw 2 shapes in the first large box. Have the children place two objects inside the first large box on their worksheet. Begin the number sentence that goes with the example by writing the numeral 2 in the first small box in the number sentence row. Have the children do the same.

- ■ Draw 2 blocks in the second large box. Have the children place 2 objects in the corresponding box on their worksheets. Write the numeral 2 in the number sentence. Have the children write a 2 in the appropriate box on their page.

- ■ Show the combination of these sets by sweeping the 4 counters into their answer boxes. Write 4 in the answer box of the number sentence and have children do the same. Read the number sentence and review the action with the children.

Note: This student worksheet should be laminated, and children should use a water soluble pen. Then many examples can be done with the same page. Children wipe off each number sentence after it has been checked.

Addition Sheet: Writing Number Sentences About Addition

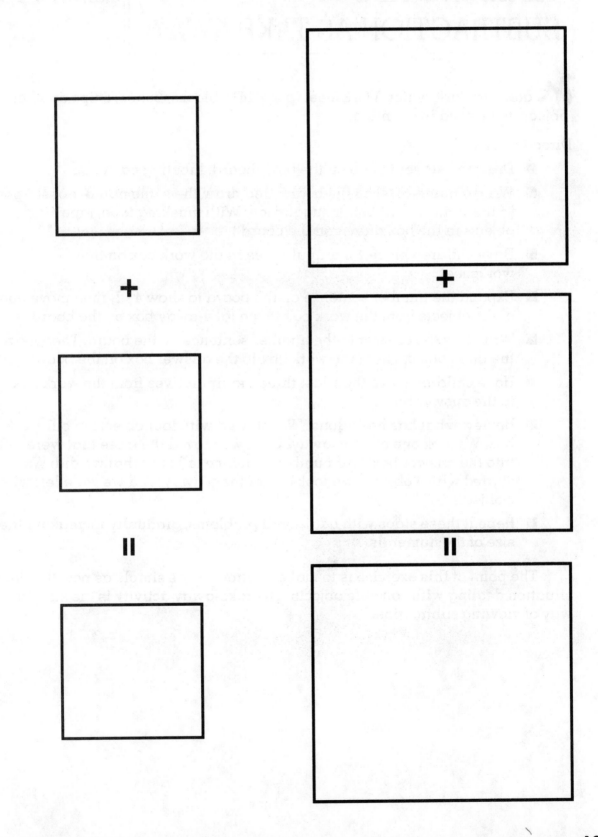

Transitional Activities

LEARNING ABOUT SUBTRACTION AS TAKE AWAY

ACTIVITY 71

𝓜 *aterials*: Subtraction Worksheet (page 141), blocks, beans, chips or other objects to be used in counting.

Directions:

■ Draw the student page on the blackboard, labeling each box.

■ Write a numeral (4) on the board, and draw the same number of shapes in the work box. (A better suggestion: With masking tape, tape 4 objects in the box drawn on the board.)

■ Have children place 4 manipulatives in the work box on their worksheet.

■ Expand the number sentence on the board to show 4 - 1, then move one of the objects from the work box to the take-away box on the board.

■ Write 3 as the answer to the number sentence on the board. Then move the three objects from the work box to the answer box on the board.

■ Have children move their last three manipulatives from the work box to the answer box.

■ Review what has been done. "We started with four objects in our work box. We took one of them away. Then we moved the three that were left into the answer box. Our number sentence tells us what we did: We started with 4 objects, we took one of them away, and we were left with 3 objects."

■ Repeat these steps with additional problems, gradually increasing the size of the numerals.

The point of this exercise is to make subtraction as simple as possible in a situation dealing with concrete objects. The take-away activity is the simplest way of viewing subtraction.

From *Primary Problem Solving in Math* by Jack A. Coffland and Gilbert J. Cuevas. Copyright © 1992 by GoodYearBooks.

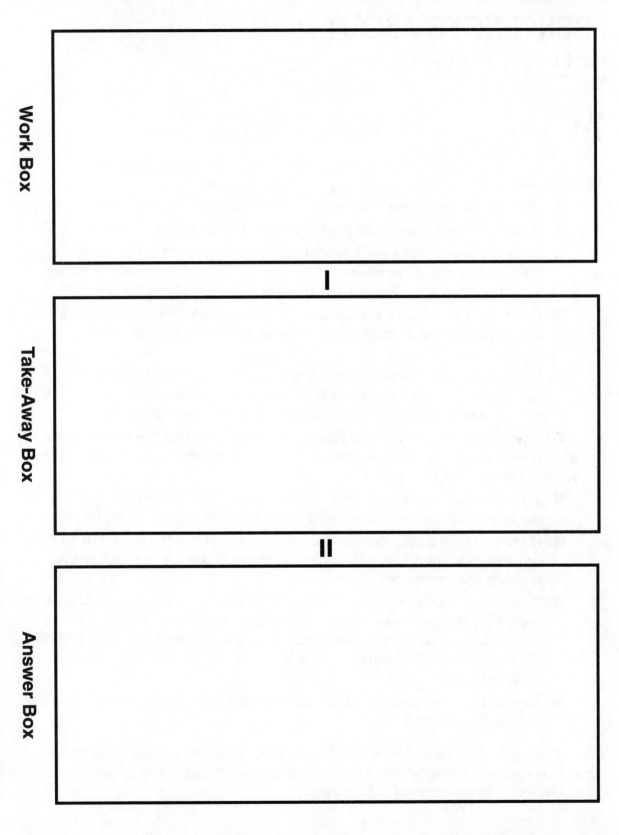

Work Box

Take-Away Box

Answer Box

BUILDING NUMBER SENTENCES ABOUT SUBTRACTION

Materials: Subtraction Worksheet (page 143), blocks, beans, chips, or other objects to be used in counting.

Directions:

■ Have students cut out numerals at the bottom of the worksheet.

■ Draw the student page on the blackboard, labeling each box.

■ Draw 5 objects in the work box on the board, and write the numeral 5 in the first box of the number sentence row. (A better suggestion: With masking tape, tape 5 objects in the work box drawn on the board.)

■ Have children place 5 manipulatives in the work box on their work sheet. Then have them place the numeral 5 in the first box of the number sentence row.

■ Expand the number sentence on the board to show 5 - 2; move two of the objects from the work box to the take-away box on the board. Then write the numeral 2 in the second box of the number sentence row.

■ Have children move two of their manipulatives from the work box to the take away box. Have them insert the numeral 2 into the second box of the number sentence row.

■ Write 3 as the answer to the number sentence on the board. Then move the three objects from the work box to the answer box on the board.

■ Have children move the three manipulatives from the work box to the answer box. Then insert the numeral three in the answer box of the number sentence row.

■ Review what work has been done. "We started with five objects in our work box. We took two of them away. Then we moved the three that were left into the answer box. Our number sentence tells what we did: We started with 5 objects, we took 2 of them away, and we were left with 3 objects."

■ Repeat these steps with additional problems, gradually increasing the size of the numerals.

The point of this exercise is to pair the manipulation of concrete objects with the number sentence in the simplest manner. The take-away activity is the simplest way of viewing subtraction.

From *Primary Problem Solving in Math* by Jack A. Coffland and Gilbert J. Cuevas. Copyright © 1992 by GoodYearBooks.

Activity Sheet: Building Number Sentences About Subtraction

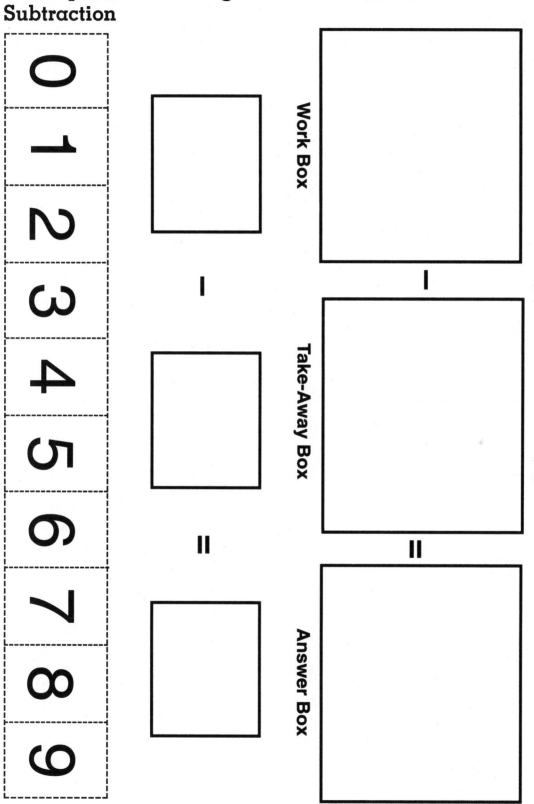

0 1 2 3 4 5 6 7 8 9

Work Box

Take-Away Box

Answer Box

−

=

PRACTICE WITH ADDITION   ACTIVITY **73**

▷ In addition, sets are combined to make one new, larger set.

To add the sets of teddy bears, we combine them

3 teddy bears
+ 2 teddy bears
_____
How many teddy bears all together?

The words tell us to put all the teddy bears together.

1.   4 apples

   + 1 apple

   _____
   How many apples all together?

2.   2 toy cars

   + 2 toy cars

   _____
   How many toy cars in all?

3.   3 turtles

   + 1 turtle

   _____
   What is the total number of turtles?

Transitional Activities

From *Primary Problem Solving in Math* by Jack A. Coffland and Gilbert J. Cuevas. Copyright © 1992 by GoodYearBooks.

Name _____   Date _____

PRACTICE WITH SUBTRACTION

 When we subtract, we take away part of a set.

Think of a set of 3 ducks.   3 ducks

Now two ducks leave.   - 2 ducks

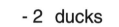

How many ducks are left?

Move 2 ducks away from the original set. 1 duck remains.

1.   4 strawberries

    - 3 strawberries
    _____

    How many strawberries are left?

2.   2 dogs

    - 2 dogs
    _____

    How many dogs are left?

3.   3 cats

    -1 cat
    _____

    How many cats are left?

| ADDING AND SUBTRACTING TOGETHER | ACTIVITY 75 |

Addition is combining sets.

   3 dolls
+ 2 dolls
_____
   5 dolls all together

A picture for this problem would show a set of 3 dolls and a set of 2 dolls being combined. The new set would have 5 dolls.

Subtraction is taking away part of a set.

   5 apples
- 1 apple that I ate
_____
   4 apples left

A picture for this problem would show five apples. Then one of the apples would be taken away. 4 apples would be left.

Draw pictures for these problems.

1.   4 oranges
   + 2 oranges
   _____
        How amny oranges in all?

2.   6 cats
   - 3 cats
   _____
        How many cats are left?

3.   7 boats
   - 3 boats
   _____
        How many boats remain?

4.   2 pennies
   + 4 pennies
   _____
        How many pennies all together?

LABELING ANSWERS

▷ People don't usually use a number all by itself. Instead of saying just 5, for example, they include what they mean by 5—say 5 fingers or 5 toy trucks. In math it is important to say what the number means. These labels tell other people what the number is about.

I have: 2 toy planes

+ 5 more toy planes
_____

How many toy planes do I have?

I have 7 toy planes.

This is called "labeling your answer."

Work these problems and label your answers.

1. 9 pet snakes

- 7 pet snakes you gave away
_____

How many snakes are left? ____ _____

2. 7 marbles

+ 12 marbles you won
_____

How many marbles do you now have? ____ _____

3. 15 lollipops

- 12 lollipops you ate
_____

How many lollipops are left? ____ _____

4. 16 baseball cards

+ 3 more baseball cards you got
_____

How many baseball cards in all? ____ _____

PICTURING PROBLEMS

ACTIVITY 77

 Directions:

Color 4 of the blocks BLUE.
Color 2 of the blocks RED.
Color 3 of the blocks GREEN.

Use the picture as you solve the problems.

1. 4 blue blocks
    + 2 red blocks
    _____
        blue and red blocks
        all together.

2. 3 green blocks
    + 2 red blocks
    _____
        green and red blocks
        blocks in all.

3. 4 blue blocks
    - 2 blue blocks
    _____
        blocks are left.

4. 3 green blocks
    - 1 green block
    _____
        blocks are left.

5. 2 red blocks
    + 4 blue blocks
    _____
        red and blue blocks
        all together.

6. 2 red blocks
    -2 red blocks
    _____
        blocks are left.

Name _____ Date _____

THINKING ABOUT MATH QUESTIONS—ADDING

You know that when we add, we put sets together to make a new, larger set. Many addition problems have questions that tell you to add. For example:

3 dogs + 4 cats

How many animals do you have in all?

The question tells you to think about "how many animals will there be after you combine the two sets?" You have to add.

Do these problems. Read each question carefully and be ready to tell what the question is asking you to think about.

1.   3 cows
    + 4 cows
    _____
        How many cows
        all together?

2.   5 stamps
    + 3 stamps
    _____
        What is the total number
        of stamps?

3.   1 toy boat
    + 3 toy boats
    _____
        How many toy boats in all?

4.   6 teddy bears
    + 2 teddy bears
    _____
        What is the total number
        of teddy bears?

5.   3 boys
    + 3 boys
    _____
        How many boys
        all together?

6.   2 TV sets
    + 1 TV set
    _____
        How many TV sets in all?

Transitional Activities

THINKING ABOUT MATH QUESTIONS—SUBTRACTING

You know that when we subtract, we take part of a set away to make a new, smaller set. A subtraction problem might have a question that tells you to subtract. Look at this example:

    5 records
 - 1 record that is broken
 _____
    How many records are left?

The question tells you to think about how many records are left after the 3 broken records are taken away. Since part of the set is taken away, you are looking for a new, smaller set. You have to subtract.

Do these problems. Read each question carefully and be ready to tell what the question is asking you to think about.

1.   6 horses
  - 3 horses run away
  _____
     How many horses are left?

2.   4 shirts
  - 1 shirt that is torn
  _____
     How many shirts are not torn?

3.   7 paper clips
  - 3 paper clips I used
  _____
     How many paper clips do you have now?

4.   6 pencils
  - 4 pencils I lost
  _____
     How many pencils are left?

5.   3 sheets of paper
  - 1 sheet that is used
  _____
     How many sheets are not used?

6.   7 chairs
  - 5 chairs that are broken
  _____
     How many chairs are not broken?

WHAT'S THE RIGHT SIGN?

▷ Questions in story problems help you to discover solutions. Some questions will tell you to subtract and others will tell you to add. Here are examples:

8 pieces of candy in a bag	4 coins in a pocket
□ 3 pieces of candy are eaten	□ 3 coins in a purse
How many pieces of candy are left?	How many coins are there all together?

But the signs on math problems are very important, too. They also tell you how to solve the problems.

What sign goes in the box? Read the question. It says "How many pieces of candy are left?" Some of the candy was eaten. Some of it was taken away. You must subtract to find what is left.

What sign goes in the box? Read the question. It asks "How many coins are there in all?" You must be combining sets to find a new, larger set. You have to add.

The problems below do not have signs. Read the questions and decide whether to add or subtract. Write the sign in the □ and solve each problem.

1. 8 gold stars
    □ 4 more gold stars
    How many gold stars do you have in all?

2. 9 clean shoes
    □ 5 shoes that got dirty
    How many shoes are still clean?

PRACTICE MAKES PERFECT

ACTIVITY **81**

▷ Read the questions and decide which sign to use. Then solve the problem.

1. 7 apples
    ☐ 4 more apples
    _____
    How many apples in all?

2. 8 tigers
    ☐ 4 tigers that run away
    _____
    How many tigers are left?

3. 9 ducks
    ☐ 8 more ducks
    _____
    How many ducks in all?

4. 18 toy cars
    ☐ 12 toy cars you give away
    _____
    How many toy cars are left?

5. 15 bananas
    ☐ 11 bananas you eat
    _____
    How many bananas remain?

6. 12 baseballs
    ☐ 4 baseballs that you lost
    _____
    How many baseballs do you have now?

7. 12 trucks
    ☐ 14 more trucks
    _____
    How many trucks in all?

8. 15 lions in the circus
    ☐ 9 lions that go to the zoo
    _____
    How many lions are still in the circus?

9. 14 dogs
    ☐ 8 more dogs
    _____
    How many dogs in all?

10. 12 basketballs
    ☐ 14 more basketballs
    _____
    How many basketballs in total?

From *Primary Problem Solving in Math* by Jack A. Coffland and Gilbert J. Cuevas. Copyright © 1992 by GoodYearBooks.

FOLLOWING DIRECTIONS

▶ Use the picture to answer these questions.

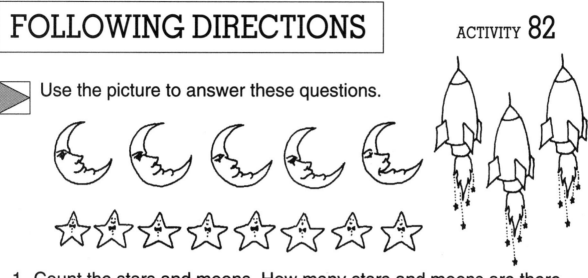

1. Count the stars and moons. How many stars and moons are there in all?

2. Jennie covers up 3 stars. How many can she see now?

3. Count the rocket ships and moons. How many rocket ships and moons are there in all?

4. Color 3 of the moons yellow. How many are not colored?

5. Color 2 of the stars blue. How many are not colored?

6. How many moons and stars have you colored so far?

7. Color all the rest of the pictures. How many things did you color in all?

From *Primary Problem Solving in Math* by Jack A. Coffland and Gilbert J. Cuevas. Copyright © 1992 by GoodYearBooks.

Chapter 5

INFORMATION GATHERING
AND PROCESSING ACTIVITIES

Information Gathering and Processing Activities

The ability to solve problems depends on the interaction of many skills. *Information-gathering and processing skills* are central to the problem-solving process. This chapter focuses on these skills. Activities are designed to help children:

■ read a problem so that it can be understood and eventually solved,

■ develop proficiency in a variety of reading skills related to problem solving,

■ identify and organize the information given in a problem, and

■ relate the information given in the problem to the mathematical process required for the solution.

Sample Activities:

> Kindergarten children draw a picture about two, describing how the number 2 can be found in everyday things.

> Third-grade children read a problem stem and write questions which are appropriate for the information given in the stem.

Instructional Considerations

When teaching children to read and analyze word problems, these general suggestions should be considered:

1. Allow children sufficient time to read the problem.
2. Use questions to guide children through the information presented in the problem.
3. Make use of manipulative materials, pictures, and charts to help children visualize the problem situation and solution process.
4. Watch out for "key words." There are both benefits and dangers involved in teaching them. A better suggestion is to deal with vocabulary in the context of the problem. Focus on identifying and defining words that play a role in the problem's solution.

5. Provide practice activities on the specifics of reading a mathematical problem statement. These skills are not always the same as reading a story from a reading textbook.

6. Take steps to ensure that children relate the numerals they use to real-life situations.

7. Structure instructional experiences so that children express mathematical ideas in their own words and phrases.

Activity Objectives

The teaching suggestions and activities are designed to help students:

- Develop the ability to understand vocabulary used in a problem by recognizing and reading all the words it contains and defining difficult and/or unfamiliar terms.

- Identify relevant facts which are helpful in solving the problem.

- Identify and interpret the question given in a problem.

- Sort out unnecessary information given in a problem; identify missing information.

- Convert a verbal statement to a numerical expression.

- Translate a numerical statement to a verbal one.

- Identify numerical statements which solve a given problem.

- Identify the appropriate pictorial model for the solution of the problem.

LINKING NUMBERS WITH EXPERIENCE

ACTIVITY **83**

Children need to link numbers with experience; they must understand that numerals are used all day long, not just in math class. One way to address these needs is to have children tell their own number experiences.

Write the "given" numeral or numerical expression on the board.

1. Given: **2**   Have the child tell personal stories about two.

   Examples: "I have two brothers."

   "My sister is two years old."

   "I got two presents for my birthday."

2. Given: **3**   Carry out a role-playing situation about three.

   Examples: "There are three boys with red shirts. Let's have them all come to the front of the room."

   "Tyrone can choose three people to play a game."

   "We have three swings. Let's pick three people so we can have a person in each swing."

3. Given: **4**   Have the child draw a picture telling about four.

   Examples: Pictures will vary. Have children tell about their pictures, then write or dictate a short sentence about it and the numeral being used.

4. Given: **2, 3** Have children tell about two different numerals.

   Examples: "I have two sisters and three brothers."

   "We have two dogs and three cats."

   "There are two boys and three girls at my table."

From *Primary Problem Solving in Math* by Jack A. Coffland and Gilbert J. Cuevas. Copyright © 1992 by GoodYearBooks.

Information Gathering and Processing Activities

5. Given: **2 + 3 = 5** Have children tell about a number sentence.

   Examples: "We have two dogs and three cats. That makes five pets."

   "There are two girls and three boys at my table. That makes five people."

   "I have two dimes. Mom gave me three more. Now I have five dimes."

6. Given: **4 - 3 = 1** Have children describe different subtraction model situations.

   Example: "I had four apples. I gave away three. Now I have one left."

   Example: "Joan has four dolls. Mary has three dolls. That means that Joan has one more doll than Mary."

7. Given the number sentence **2 + 4 = 6**, tell a story about it.

   "I have two candy bars. I get four more candy bars. Then I have six candy bars in all."

   Collect children's stories and write them as language experience charts. Read them with children several times over a period of several days. The charts might also be used as bulletin boards later in the year.

8. Given a number sentence, draw a picture about the sentence.

9. Given a number sentence, role play the situation it could describe.

10. Discuss numbers orally in class whenever possible.

MAKING COMPARISONS

*O*ne special aspect of the mathematical vocabulary is the language used to make *comparisons*. Use the Making Comparisons Worksheet on page 161 for the following activities.

a. The concept of "the same number as"

■ Have the students place 2 blocks in the rectangle.

■ Direct children to place *the same number of blocks* in the circle.

■ Have different children answer these questions:

How many blocks did you put in the rectangle?
How many blocks did you put in the circle?
Which has more blocks, the circle or the rectangle?
Why?

b. The concept of "one more than"

■ Have the students place 3 blocks in the rectangle.

■ Direct the children to place *one more than* 3 blocks in the circle.

■ Have different children answer these questions:

How many blocks did you put in the rectangle?
How many blocks did you put in the circle?
Which has more blocks, the circle or the rectangle?
How many more?

c. The concept of "one less than"

■ Have the students place 5 blocks in the rectangle.

■ Direct the children to place *one less than* 5 blocks in the circle.

■ Have different children answer these questions:

How many blocks did you put in the rectangle?
How many blocks did you put in the circle?
Which has less blocks, the circle or the rectangle?
How many less?

d. Repeat activities like these often with different quantities.

From *Primary Problem Solving in Math* by Jack A. Coffland and Gilbert J. Cuevas. Copyright © 1992 by GoodYearBooks.

Activity Sheet: Making Comparisons

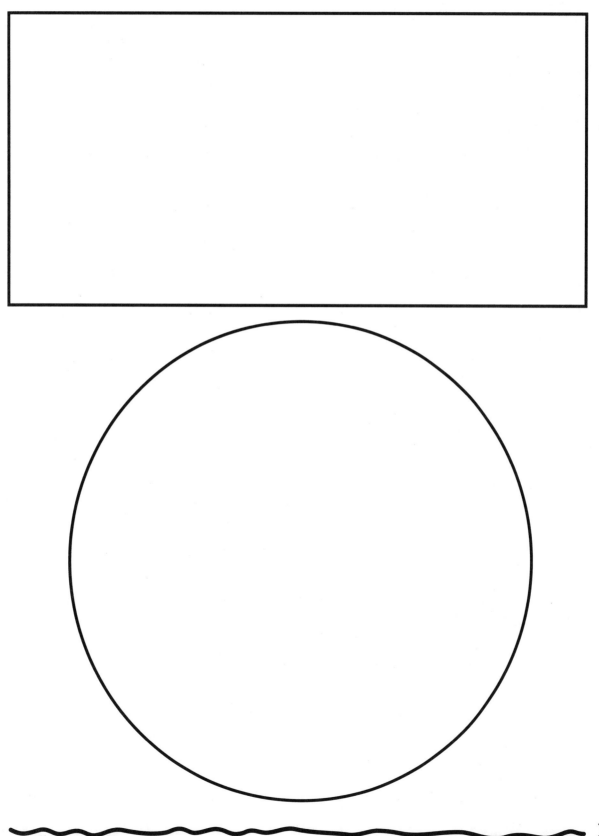

MAKING NUMERICAL COMPARISONS

ACTIVITY 85

Help children use the worksheet on page 163 as you lead the following activities.

a. The concept of "same number" or "just as many"

■ Have the students place 4 blocks in the rectangle.

■ Direct the children to place the same number in the circle.

■ Ask: How many blocks did you put in the rectangle?
How many blocks did you put in the circle?
Tell me what you just did.

Vary the exercise with the phrase "just as many." Repeat often, using different numerals each time. Use 1 - 5 for all the beginning exercises; gradually move on to larger numerals.

b. The concept of "all"

■ Have the students put 3 blocks in the rectangle.

■ Direct the children to move all of the blocks to the circle.

■ Ask: How many blocks did you put in the rectangle?
How many blocks did you move to the circle?
How many blocks are left in the rectangle now?

c. The concept of "some"

■ Have the children put 4 blocks in the rectangle.

■ Direct the students to move some of them to the circle.

■ Ask: How many blocks did you put in the rectangle?
How many blocks did you move to the circle?
How many blocks are left in the rectangle now?

d. The concept of the "same/different number"

■ Have the students put 2 blocks in the rectangle.

■ Direct the children to put the same/different number in the circle.

■ Ask: How many blocks did you put in the rectangle?
How many blocks did you move to the circle?
Do you have the same number or a different number of blocks in the shapes?

From *Primary Problem Solving in Math* by Jack A. Coffland and Gilbert J. Cuevas. Copyright © 1992 by GoodYearBooks.

Information Gathering and Processing Activities

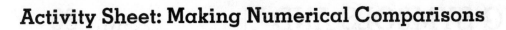

Activity Sheet: Making Numerical Comparisons

LINKING SYMBOLS AND WORDS IN ADDITION

In helping children understand the words and amounts used in addition number sentences, offer the following directions:

- ■ Copy the worksheet on page 168, and have students cut out the number words.

- ■ Draw the student page (page 165) on the chalkboard.

- ■ Draw (or place with masking tape) 3 objects in the first box.

- ■ Have students put that same number of counters in the first box at the top of the page.

- ■ Then have students find the word "three" to place in the first box of the bottom row.

- ■ Repeat with the second pair of boxes. Put 2 objects in the top row; have students do the same. Then have students find the word "two" and place it in the second row.

- ■ Then ask students to "sweep" all the concrete objects together into the answer box. There should be five. Then ask students to find the word "five" and place it in the answer box on the bottom row.

- ■ Review: We have combined a set of 3 and 2 to make 5, and we have shown the words which tell us that "three + two = five".

- ■ Repeat with additional examples.

From *Primary Problem Solving in Math* by Jack A. Coffland and Gilbert J. Cuevas. Copyright © 1992 by GoodYearBooks.

Activity Sheet: Linking Symbols and Words in Addition

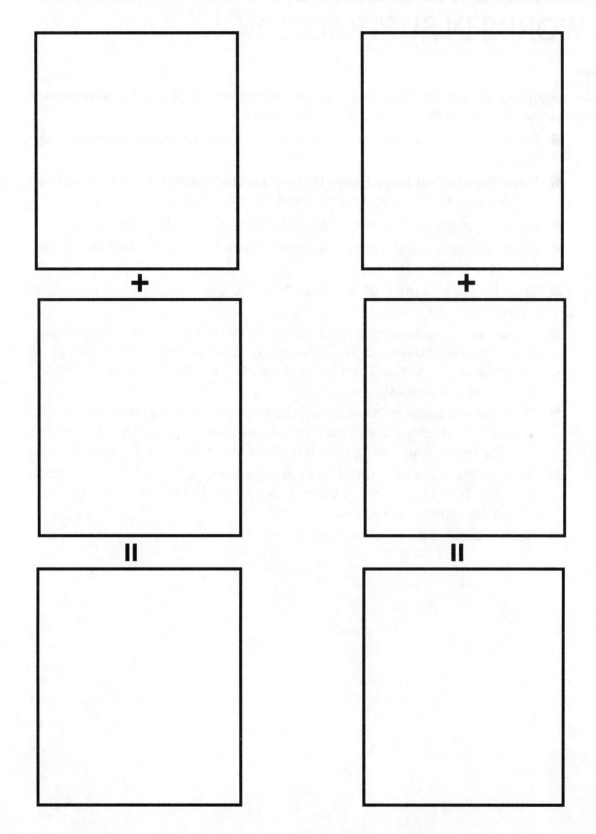

LINKING SYMBOLS AND WORDS IN SUBTRACTION

ACTIVITY 87

I n helping children understand the words and amounts used in subtraction number sentences, offer the following directions:

- ■ Have students cut out the number words from the worksheet on page 168.

- ■ Draw the student page (page 167) on the chalkboard. Label the boxes as "work box", "take-away box" and "answer box".

- ■ Draw (or place with masking tape) 5 objects in the first box.

- ■ Have students put that same number of counters in the first box at the top of the page.

- ■ Then have students find the word "five" to place in the work box on the bottom row.

- ■ Repeat with the second pair of boxes. Take away 1 object (by moving one of the five objects to the "take-away" box) in the top row; have students do the same. Then have students find the word "one" and place it in the second row.

- ■ Then ask students to "sweep" all the concrete objects left in the work box into the answer box. There should be four. Then ask students to find the word "four" and place it in the answer box on the bottom row.

- ■ Review: We have combined a set of 5, and we took 1 object away from that wet. We are left with a set of 4. We have shown the words which tell us that "five - one = four".

- ■ Repeat with additional examples.

From *Primary Problem Solving in Math* by Jack A. Coffland and Gilbert J. Cuevas. Copyright © 1992 by GoodYearBooks.

Information Gathering and Processing Activities

Activity Sheet: Linking Symbols and Words in Subtraction

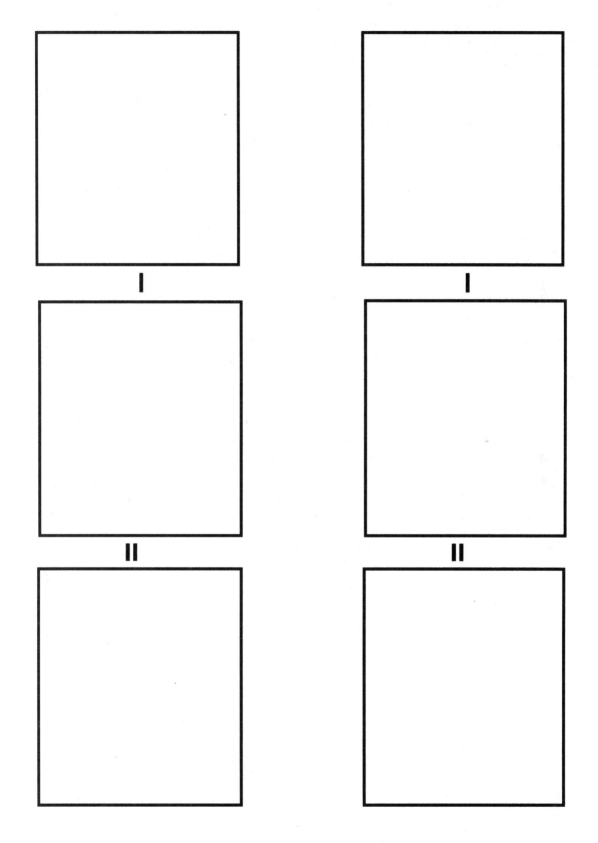

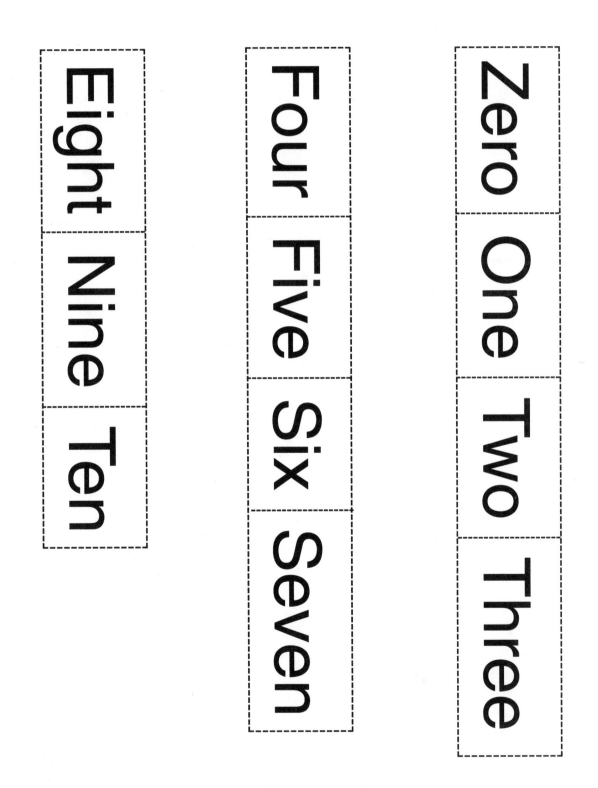

Zero One Two Three

Four Five Six Seven

Eight Nine Ten

MATH WORD SEARCH 1

ACTIVITY **88**

Math words are hidden in these puzzles. To find them you must look across or up and down or diagonally. Some of the words are even given backwards. See if you can find all the words on each list.

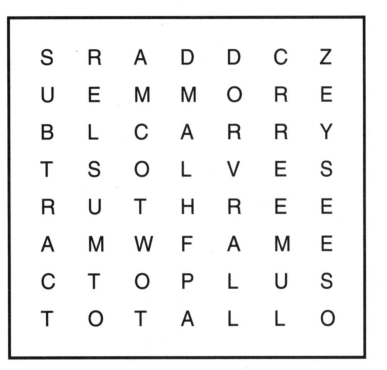

```
S   R   A   D   D   C   Z
U   E   M   M   O   R   E
B   L   C   A   R   R   Y
T   S   O   L   V   E   S
R   U   T   H   R   E   E
A   M   W   F   A   M   E
C   T   O   P   L   U   S
T   O   T   A   L   L   O
```

Words to Find

subtract   carry   plus

sum   three   total

add   two   more

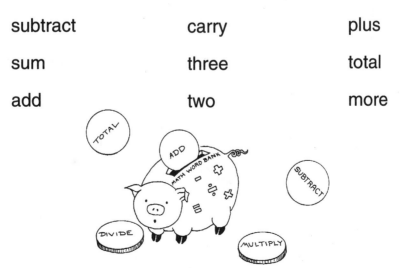

From *Primary Problem Solving in Math* by Jack A. Coffland and Gilbert J. Cuevas. Copyright © 1992 by GoodYearBooks.

MATH WORD SEARCH 2   ACTIVITY 89

Math words are hidden in these puzzles. To find them you must look across or up and down or diagonally. Some of the words are even given backwards. See if you can find all the words on each list.

```
A   F   O   O   T   O   P
D   E   N   B   I   M   O
I   N   C   H   M   I   U
S   A   L   L   E   L   N
T   X   S   P   E   E   D
A   O   L   I   N   D   O
N   R   N   N   E   W   L
C   B   E   T   O   L   L
E   R   Y   A   R   D   A
G   A   L   L   O   N   R
```

Measurement Words

ton	inch	dollar	mile
foot	time	gallon	
pound	speed	area	
distance	pint	yard	

Information Gathering and Processing Activities

From *Primary Problem Solving in Math* by Jack A. Coffland and Gilbert J. Cuevas. Copyright © 1992 by GoodYearBooks.

WHAT DOESN'T BELONG?

ACTIVITY **90**

▷ Here are fifteen sets of math words or phrases. In each set there is one word or phrase that does not belong. Circle the word that does not belong.

1. add	addition	take-away	combine sets
2. take-away	add	less	minus
3. pint	gallon	subtract	quart
4. circle	round	straight line	curved line
5. square	rectangle	triangle	four sides
6. one	ten	one half	twenty
7. ten's place	number	triangle	place value
8. all together	together	add to	left over
9. sum	take-away	less	difference
10. square	curved line	straight line	triangle
11. dollar	multiply	quarter	dime
12. length	distance	yard	penny
13. greater than	equal to	four	less than
14. four	ten	five	six
15. hour	mile	gallon	take-away

A MATH WORD SEARCH I AND II, WHAT DOESN'T BELONG

ACTIVITIES **88,** **89,** AND **90**

Building Math Vocabulary

Mathematics has a special language of its own. Many of the terms are specialized, rarely used in day-to-day conversations. Other mathematical terms may be common words used in uncommon ways. Students have several problems in reading mathematical text, including such difficulties as reading/recognizing mathematical terms, knowing what those terms mean, determining how to interpret them, and deciding how to use the information given to solve the problem.

Activities for overcoming these difficulties can be integrated into either the math period or the language arts period of the school day. (These activities do not always need to be packed into the mathematics lesson!) Incorporating math activities into the language arts period will communicate to students that "math ideas" may be found in any subject taught during the day.

The main goal of vocabulary development activities in math is to have students *recognize and understand mathematical terms and symbols in context.* Although terms may be presented in isolation during the early stages of mathematical language development, eventually these terms must be used and understood within broader contexts.

Many times students do not realize that words may have mathematical meaning when used in context with other words.

Provide practice for children in recognizing these words through exercises like "What Doesn't Belong?" (page 171). Here, four words are provided in each list; students should see that three of the words are related in some fashion; one word does not belong.

Discuss the meaning of each word and the relationship which exists between three words in each row. Discuss why the fourth does not belong.

Answers to Activity 90:

1. take-away
2. add
3. subtract
4. straight line
5. triangle
6. one half
7. triangle
8. left over
9. sum
10. curved line
11. multiply
12. penny
13. four
14. five
15. take-away

ANOTHER KIND OF WORD SEARCH

▷ Underline the words in this story which could have math meanings.

Betsy has a large animal farm. One morning she found a break in the fence around her farm. She measured the break to be twelve feet long. Now she knew why she had lost four sheep, two deer, and two dozen chickens. She pulled a piece of paper and a pencil from her pocket. She wrote: "First, buy twelve feet of wire. Second, fix the fence." She needed to get the fence repaired by noon the next day. She was going to get a dozen horses. She did not want to lose any more animals.

From *Primary Problem Solving in Math* by Jack A. Coffland and Gilbert J. Cuevas. Copyright © 1992 by GoodYearBooks.

ANOTHER KIND OF WORD SEARCH

*O*ne good way to help students realize how we use mathematical terms in everyday language is to read a story or a section of prose that includes the use of math words. Ask students to find those words. The text may come from a library book, a section of your social studies book, a newspaper, etc. Words in the following selection do have or might have math meanings.

> Betsy has a *large* animal farm. One morning she found a break in the fence *around* her farm. She *measured* the break to be *twelve feet long*. Now she knew why she had lost *four* sheep, *two* deer, and *two dozen* chickens. She pulled a piece of paper and a pencil from her pocket. She wrote: "*First*, buy *twelve feet* of wire. *Second*, fix the fence." She needed to get the fence repaired by *noon* the *next day*. She was going to get a *dozen* horses. She did not want to lose any *more* animals.

Repeat this activity with other reading selections.

CREATING SENTENCES WITH MATH WORDS

ACTIVITY **92**

▷ Here is a list of words you are likely to find in a math book. Put each one in a sentence.

MATH WORD BANK

SUBTRACT
ADD
SUM
MULTIPLY
DIVIDE
TOTAL

Example: More
I have more marbles than you do.

1. Sum _____.

2. Addition _____.

3. Total _____.

4. Difference _____.

5. Minus _____.

6. Circle _____.

7. First _____.

8. Nine _____.

9. Square _____.

10. More than _____.

CREATING SENTENCES WITH MATH WORDS

*E*mphasis must be given to the understanding of "mathematical words" in context. Once students have had some experiences with the terms they may encounter in word problems, determine if the students can use them in meaningful sentences.

After students have completed the worksheet for this activity (page 175), ask several of them to write their sentences on the board (or write them yourself as students say them). Discuss how some students remained close to the mathematical context (i.e., "three minus two equals one") while others may have attempted to use these words in the context of everyday communication (i.e., "I had a total of three pencils when I left for school."). Emphasize the fact that the words have numerical meanings in both contexts.

OUT OF THIS WORLD

ACTIVITY **93**

▷ Write a short answer to each question.

SATELLITE ELEMENTARY SCHOOL
BLAST-OFF BAKE SALE
WEDNESDAY, NOVEMBER 17, 1999
ASTEROID COOKIES.....5¢
ALIEN BROWNIES.....10¢
ROCKET CUPCAKES.....5¢
MARTIAN WAFFLES....25¢
THE SALE WILL BE HELD FROM 2:15 PM UNTIL 4:00 PM

1. What is the advertisement for?

2. When does it take place? Where does it take place?

3. What is being sold?

4. How much are the:
   a. cookies?   c. cupcakes?

   b. brownies?   d. waffles?

5. Can I buy a Martian waffle with 10¢? with $1.00?

6. Can I get a cookie for my friend if I only have 5¢?

OUT OF THIS WORLD

ACTIVITY 93

Reading for detail is an important part of problem solving. Unlike reading class activities which often are designed to find the main idea or the major generalization, reading activities in the math class must focus on the meaning of one word or discovering an important detail. Frequent opportunities for this sort of reading will be necessary in a math problem-solving program.

You can lead many activities which will provide students with experiences in finding and remembering specific information about a problem setting. The following is an example:

Write the following information on the chalkboard.

SATELLITE ELEMENTARY SCHOOL
BLAST-OFF BAKE SALE
WEDNESDAY, NOVEMBER 17, 1999
ASTEROID COOKIES......5¢
ALIEN BROWNIES......10¢
ROCKET CUPCAKES......5¢
MARTIAN WAFFLES....25¢
THE SALE WILL BE HELD FROM 2:15 PM UNTIL 4:00 PM

Sample questions to ask students:

1. What is happening? What is this ad for?
2. When does it take place? Where does it take place?
3. What is being sold?
4. How much are the cookies/brownies/cupcakes/waffles?
5. Can I buy a Martian waffle with 10¢? with $1.00?
6. Can I get a cookie for my friend if I only have 5¢?

Extension:
Have the students create their own "information posters." These can be displayed and questions posed that dea with the information on the poster.

SALE MAIL

▷ Read the sale flyer below.

Widgets "R" Us
SALE
ONLY TODAY
ONE SMALL WIDGET. . . . . 10¢
ONE BIG WIDGET. . . . . 15¢
ONE SMALL GADGET. . . . . . . 12¢
ONE BIG GADGET. . . . . 30¢

Circle the correct answer.

1. Where is the sale taking place?
   a. at a toy store
   b. at a hardware store
   c. at a widget store
   d. at a drugstore

2. When is the sale taking place?
   a. May 23, 1998
   b. Tuesday
   c. November
   d. I can't tell

3. Can you buy a small widget with a quarter? Yes No

4. Can you buy a large gadget with 12¢? Yes No

5. Can you buy two small widgets with 30¢? Yes No

6. Does a large widget cost more than a large gadget? Yes No

7. Can you buy a large gadget with a dime? Yes No

8. You bought a small widget. You paid for it with 15¢.
   Will you get change back? Yes No

9. You went into the store with 50¢. You want to buy
   all four items. Can you? Yes No

10. You went into the store with 75¢. You bought all
    four items. Will you get change? Yes No

READ ALL ABOUT IT!   ACTIVITY 95

▶ Read the poster. Then answer the questions.

Roller Skating Party

Saturday, May 23, 1998
Fast Wheels Roller Rink

Admission 50¢
Bring a gift to share
(DO NOT SPEND
MORE THAN $1.00)

If your last name begins with
the letter A through L
BRING A GIFT FOR A BOY

If Your last name begins with
the letter M through Z
BRING A GIFT FOR A GIRL

1. *What* is taking place?
   a. a birthday party
   b. a baseball game
   c. a skating party
   d. a swimming party

3. *Where* will it take place?
   a. at the Hot Wheels Roller Rink
   b. at the Fast Wheels Roller Rink
   c. at the For Wheels Rink
   d. I don't know.

5. What should you bring to the party?
   a. a book
   b. food
   c. a present
   d. your parents

2. *When* does it take place?
   a. Saturday, May 10, 1998
   b. Saturday, June 23, 1998
   c. Sunday, May 23, 1998
   d. Saturday, May 23, 1998

4. What is the admission charge?
   a. $1.00
   b. $0.10
   c. $0.01
   d. $0.50

6. Can you go with 75¢?
   a. Yes
   b. No
   c. What party?
   d. I was not invited.

7. Who is supposed to bring presents for the boys?
   a. people with first names starting with the letters A through L
   b. people with last names starting with the letters A through L
   c. people with first names starting with the letters M through Z
   d. people with last names starting with the letters M through Z

Name _____   Date _____

IS IT REALLY TRUE?

▶ Read this ad about a new amusement park.

Slip and Slide Water Park
NOW OPEN
Tuesday through Thursday
from 4PM until 10PM
Friday from 4PM until Midnight
Saturday from 9AM until Midnight
Sunday from 1PM until 10PM

Admission
Adults $5.00
Teenagers $3.00
Children under twelve $1.50

Decide if the sentences below are true or false. Circle your choice.

1. The water park will open next week.   True   False

2. The park is open on Sundays.   True   False

3. A third-grader must pay $3.00 to get in.   True   False

4. You can go to the park on Wednesdays at 1PM.   True   False

5. Mom and Dad can get in for $3.00.   True   False

6. The name of the Park is *Slip and Slide.*   True   False

7. You can get in if you have $2.75.   True   False

8. There are rock concerts at the park.   True   False

9. The park is open on Sundays from 2PM until 10PM.   True   False

10. The park is closed on Mondays.   True   False

"READING A PICTURE"

▷ The picture shows Miss Campo's gas station and food store.

Look at the picture. Answer the questions by circling either Yes, No, or Can't Tell.

1. Can you buy a comic book for 75¢?   Yes   No   Can't Tell

2. Is the station closed?   Yes   No   Can't Tell

3. Can you buy a newspaper with a nickel?   Yes   No   Can't Tell

4. Is the name of the station "The Last Stand"?   Yes   No   Can't Tell

5. Can you buy snacks at this station?   Yes   No   Can't Tell

6. Is there someone selling oranges?   Yes   No   Can't Tell

7. Is there a girl putting air in her bike's tire?   Yes   No   Can't Tell

8. Can you buy oil for 50¢?   Yes   No   Can't Tell

9. Is there someone in the picture paying for gas?   Yes   No   Can't Tell

10. Can you buy one soft drink if you have 50¢?   Yes   No   Can't Tell

Information Gathering and Processing Activities

Teaching Suggestions

SALE MAIL, READ ALL ABOUT IT!, IS IT REALLY TRUE?, "READING A PICTURE"

*T*he ability to read a problem and find specific information to use in its solution is a vital skill in problem solving. However, there are many children who can read the words in a problem and still not be able to find a solution.

Therefore, teachers need to pay attention to the thinking skills required to solve problems. Children must read the problem *and* make decisions about how to use the information to solve it.

Use these four activities as practice in the process of reading and interpreting information given in a problem: Sale Mail, Read All About It!, Is It Really True?, and "Reading a Picture."

From *Primary Problem Solving in Math* by Jack A. Coffland and Gilbert J. Cuevas. Copyright © 1992 by GoodYearBooks.

WHERE'S THE QUESTION?

▷ Underline the part of each of these problems that tells what you will need to do to find the answer. Then solve the problem.

1. Speedo ran 7 miles on Monday, 6 on Tuesday, and 3 on Wednesday. How many miles did he run in all?

2. If Speedo ran 6 miles on Sunday and 3 on Thursday, how many more miles did he run on Sunday than on Thursday?

3. A notebook costs 75¢, a pencil costs 25¢, and a ruler 15¢. How much do you have to pay for a ruler and a pencil?

4. Rebecca is 12 years old and Maria is 10. Who is older? How many years older?

5. Joe delivered 24, 35, and 20 newspapers on three different days last week. How many newspapers did he deliver in all?

6. If you have 25¢ and the comic book you want costs 30¢, how much more money do you need?

7. What do you have to pay if you want to buy three popsicles and each costs 20¢? How much would two popsicles cost?

8. Your class of 30 students is planning a party. You need 43 people to get a special price at the skating rink. Find out how many more students you have to invite to get the special admission price.

9. If today is February 15, how many more days are there until March 1st?

10. Shirley works in an auto parts shop. One day she unpacked three cases of oil filters. Each case has 10 filters. Find how many filters were in the cases Shirley unpacked.

From *Primary Problem Solving in Math* by Jack A. Coffland and Gilbert J. Cuevas. Copyright © 1992 by GoodYearBooks.

WHAT AM I LOOKING FOR?

ACTIVITY 99

 Read each of the following problems. Then **select the statement** that tells you what the problem question asks.

1. Your scores on last week's tests were 72, 49, 88, and 95. What was your highest score?

   The problem asks you to find

   _____ your total score

   _____ your worst score

   _____ your best score

2. Joan has 3 pennies and 4 dimes. How much **money** is that?

   The question asks you

   _____ how much money in four dimes

   _____ how much money in three pennies and four dimes

   _____ how much money Joan spent

3. Aliens visited 3 planets one week and 7 planets the next week. How many more planets did they visit the second **week**?

   To answer this problem you must find

   _____ the number of planets the aliens visited

   _____ the number of planets the aliens visited the first week

   _____ the difference between the number of planets visited during week one and week two

4. Find how much money Pablo has left from one dollar if he spent 50 cents on a comic book.

   You have to find

   _____ the number of comic books Pablo bought

   _____ the amount of money Pablo spent

   _____ the amount of money Pablo has left

From *Primary Problem Solving in Math* by Jack A. Coffland and Gilbert J. Cuevas. Copyright © 1992 by GoodYearBooks.

A QUESTION OF QUESTIONS | ACTIVITY 100

▷ Select a question that makes a math problem out of the stories below. Make sure the question you select creates a word problem that requires mathematics for a solution.

1. Bill has 7 marbles and Tony has 9.

    _____ a. How many marbles does Bill have?

    _____ b. How many marbles do they have together?

    _____ c. How many more marbles do they have than Jim?

2. Fernando's class went to the library. They checked out four mysteries, five books of science fiction, seven westerns, and two biographies.

    _____ a. How many students went to the library?

    _____ b. How many biographies were checked out?

    _____ c. How many books were checked out by the class?

3. Last week Mrs. Lewis was painting her house. She painted three rooms the first day, two the second, and four the third.

    _____ a. How many more rooms did she paint on the first day than on the second?

    _____ b. How many rooms did she paint the fourth day?

    _____ c. Who was painting the house?

4. Becky feeds all of the animals in her 4-H Club. She buys 10 sacks of pet food every week.

    _____ a. How many animals does Becky have?

    _____ b. How many sacks of food will she buy in 3 weeks?

    _____ c. How many sacks of food does she buy each week?

From *Primary Problem Solving in Math* by Jack A. Coffland and Gilbert J. Cuevas. Copyright © 1992 by GoodYearBooks.

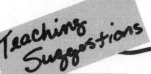

WHERE'S THE QUESTION, WHAT AM I LOOKING FOR?, AND A QUESTION OF QUESTIONS

ACTIVITIES **98, 99,** AND **100**

*T*he question posed in a word problem is an essential component of the solution. It tells you what you must find or what must be done to obtain an answer. Children often have difficulty dealing with questions. The information presented in the problem statement may be identified correctly, but students may experience an inability to determine what is being asked, and/or link the question to the information presented.

It is important for children to spend time reading and examining different problem questions to see how they relate to the solution. To introduce these activity pages, you may wish to use the following general strategy:

■ Read the following "story."

> Jim, Alice, and their uncle went to a football game. There were lots of people at the stadium. During the game Jim, Alice, and their uncle had 3 soft drinks, 2 bags of popcorn, and 4 hotdogs. The home team won 33 to 23. Everyone enjoyed the game.

■ Ask the class to give an answer to the problem (after all, it is a math class!). Despite the fact that there is no question, some students may come up with numerical answers—for example, "The home team won by 10 points." Other students might say that this "story" is not a math problem because it does not include a question.

■ Discuss what must be added in order to make it into a story problem. Ask students to help in deciding what should be included. Emphasize in the discussion how the question must relate to the information given in the problem.

■ Finally, ask children to read the problems on the worksheet entitled Where's the Question? Discuss how each question relates to the information in the problem.

■ The activities What Am I Looking For? and A Question of Questions also deal with finding/interpreting questions.

PUTTING IT ALL TOGETHER   ACTIVITY 101

 Read each problem. Check all of the statements needed to solve the problem.

1. There are three children in the Sanchez family. Each one wants a milk shake. What is the total cost if each milk shake costs one dollar?

_____ Three children want milk shakes.

_____ The Sanchez children want milk shakes.

_____ The milk shakes cost one dollar each.

_____ The problem asks how much a milk shake costs.

2. John weighed 53 pounds when he was in the sixth grade. In eighth grade he weighed 97 pounds. How much weight did he gain?

_____ John is now in the eighth grade.

_____ John gained weight.

_____ John weighed 53 pounds in the sixth grade.

_____ John weighed 97 pounds in the eighth grade.

3. Maria bought a tape for $3 and a poster for $4. How much money did she spend?

_____ Maria bought a tape.

_____ Maria spent $3 dollars for a tape.

_____ Maria was in the record shop.

_____ Maria had money.

_____ Maria spent $4 on a poster.

From *Primary Problem Solving in Math* by Jack A. Coffland and Gilbert J. Cuevas. Copyright © 1992 by GoodYearBooks.

4. Jimmy mowed three lawns on Monday, two on Tuesday and 4 on Wednesdays. How many lawns did he mow in all?

_____ Jimmy mowed lawns on Monday.

_____ Jimmy mowed 3 lawns on Monday.

_____ Jimmy has a yard service.

_____ Jimmy wants to know the total number of lawns he mowed.

_____ Jimmy mowed 4 lawns on Wednesday.

5. Yesterday's temperature was 80 degrees. Today the temperature is 60 degrees. How much cooler is today than yesterday?

_____ Today is Monday.

_____ The temperature yesterday was 60.

_____ The temperature today is 60.

_____ The temperature yesterday was 80.

_____ The difference between yesterday's and today's temperature.

Solve each problem in the space below.

Teaching Suggestions

PUTTING IT ALL TOGETHER

ACTIVITY 101

$\mathcal{S}$o far, students have had practice in specific reading skills needed in problem solving. Now it's time to put them all together.

The last activity worksheet in this book requires students to:

> read and comprehend all words,
> find the specific information needed to solve the problem,
> and, read and interpret the question.

Discuss this worksheet with students. Spend time on why certain information is or is not needed to solve the problem. Consider other possible questions and how they might change the problem which must be solved.